Edward Everett

Account of the Fund for the Relief of East Tennessee

Edward Everett

Account of the Fund for the Relief of East Tennessee

ISBN/EAN: 9783337398675

Printed in Europe, USA, Canada, Australia, Japan

Cover: Foto ©Suzi / pixelio.de

More available books at **www.hansebooks.com**

ACCOUNT

OF THE

FUND FOR THE RELIEF OF EAST TENNESSEE;

WITH A

COMPLETE LIST OF THE CONTRIBUTORS.

BY

EDWARD EVERETT,

CHAIRMAN OF THE COMMITTEE.

BOSTON:

LITTLE, BROWN AND COMPANY.

1864.

ACCOUNT OF THE FUND.

THE condition of East Tennessee had, from the outbreak of the war, excited much interest in the loyal States. It has sometimes been called the Switzerland of North America, and certainly no part of the continent had higher claims to the name of "the happy valley." Its fame had crossed the Atlantic. More than twenty years ago, an English gentleman, who had lived several years in East Tennessee, published a pamphlet in London, in which he expresses himself in the following glowing terms : —

"To one who has resided some years in the valley of East Tennessee, breathing the pure air from its mountains, and drinking of its crystal springs, enjoying the sunny smile of its temperature and the cooling shade of its noble forests, delighting the eye and the heart with its fields of fruitfulness, which at every turn present a new aspect, it is not 'England's laughing meads,' nor 'her flowering orchard trees,' nor yet Lomond and the Trosachs, with all their beauty and historical associations, and the magic thrown around them by the exuberant imagination of the poet, that could tempt him again to quit the peaceful solitude, the clear blue sky, the song of the mocking-bird, the note of the dove, the hum of the humming-bird, and the silence of nature where all is echo." [1]

[1] *A brief Historical, Statistical, and Descriptive Review of East Tennessee, developing its immense Agricultural, Mining, and Manufacturing Advantages.* By J. Gray Smith, a naturalized citizen of the United States. London, 1842.

Some further description of the natural features of this favored region will be found in the following pages. It is sufficient to observe here, that it was inhabited before the commencement of the war by a substantial population of about 300,000, employed chiefly in agriculture, and for the most part cultivating farms of moderate size. Although surrounded on all sides by slaveholding States, and conterminous with those in which the slaves stand in the largest proportion to the free population, less than ten per cent. of the entire population of East Tennessee are slaves. It is no doubt in a considerable degree owing to this cause, that the great majority of the people have adhered to the Union, under circumstances of unexampled trial, from the commencement of the war avowedly levied by the South for the protection, perpetuation, and extension of slavery.

By their loyalty to the Constitution and Union, the people of East Tennessee were immediately marked out as the victims of the most cruel persecution, on the part of the leaders of the Rebellion. Although the oppression of the Southern minority by the Northern numerical majority had for many years been the favorite topic of the agitators in the slaveholding States, no respect was anywhere paid to the rights of the loyal minority opposed to secession, although in East Tennessee they amounted to six-sevenths of the local population. Mr. Calhoun spent the last half of his life in contriving organic arrangements, by which a minority should possess a veto on the measures of the majority, but the moment the appeal was made to arms, the Unionists throughout the South became the victims of unrelenting proscription. Mr. Senator Mason, of Virginia, in a letter addressed by him to the editor of a public journal, declared that those who did not choose to vote for the ordinance of Secession, — obtained as it was in secret conclave by surprise, intimidation, and fraud, — must expatriate themselves; and plainly intimated that troops had already been sent from the Gulf States to compel them to do so. This sentence of banishment, for refusing to commit treason, was denounced against a third part of the population of Virginia. A correspondence which took place at the close of 1863, between Mr. Jefferson Davis and the Governor of North Carolina, has been recently brought to light, in which the Governor is rebuked for even wishing to conciliate the Unionists of that State, who are denounced as traitors by Mr. Davis, and threatened with punishment as such. The friends of the Union in all the Border States, constituting a great majority of the people, instead of being left undisturbed in their loyalty, or even permitted to enjoy in peace their rights as a minority dissenting from the policy of the slaveholding States, have been, over and over again, invaded by the armies of the South, their towns and cities sacked, their property plundered and destroyed, and their young men forced into the ranks of the enemy.

But nowhere have the rights of a dissenting minority been so flagrantly violated as in East Tennessee, whose inhabitants, owing to the isolated position of the valley, were for two long years beyond the reach of the protecting arm of the General Government. The treatment to which they have been subjected will be more fully set forth in the following pages. It is briefly summed up in a memorial to Congress of their eloquent champion, Colonel N. G. Taylor : —

" I will not say," he observes, "that they are more loyal, but I do declare that they have been more terribly and cruelly tested and tried than any other of our people. In 1861, when the question was presented, out of a vote of little more than 40,000, they gave 30,000 majority for the Union. Their arms and ammunition were seized, before they could organize, by the rebel soldiers ; and though the Government, which owed them protection, did not protect them, yet their hearts clung to the Government, and they prayed for the Union. Five thousand of their men have seen the inside walls of rebel prisons, and hundreds of them, covered with filth, devoured of vermin, famished with hunger, have died martyrs to their country there. Their property has been seized, confiscated ; their houses pillaged ; their stock all driven off; their grain consumed, their substance wasted, their fences burned, their fields laid waste, their farms devastated by friends as well as foes. The Rebels robbed them, the Federals devoured them, for they had short supplies, and our women broke their last biscuit and gave them the biggest half, out of the mouths of hungry children. They gave up the last horse, mule, cow, sheep, hog, everything they had, to the soldiers that needed them, because they were Union. soldiers, or were plundered of them by the enemy. Their young men have been hunted like wild beasts, by soldiers, by Indians, sometimes by bloodhounds, and, when caught, tied two-and-two to long ropes, and driven before cavalry — thin-clad, barefooted, and bleeding — over frozen roads and icy creeks and rivers. Some have been beaten with ropes, with straps, with clubs. Some have been butchered, others shot down, in their own houses or yards, in the high road, or the field, or in the forest ; others, still, have been hung up by the neck to the limbs of trees, without judge or jury. I have heard of no single neighborhood within the bounds of East Tennessee, whose green sod has not drunk the blood of citizens murdered."

Such was the respect paid by the leaders of the Rebellion to the rights of their fellow-citizens who chose to adhere to the Union. Even the liberating army of the General Government did, at first, but complete the exhaustion of the devoted region, for in his haste to expel the enemy, General Burnside was compelled to move in advance of his supplies. As soon as a communication was open with the North, a cry for relief went forth from our afflicted fellow-citizens of East Tennessee. Colonel Taylor, of Carter County, who had formerly represented them in Congress, — a victim himself of the· devastations he has so feelingly described, — was deputed to visit the Northern cities, where he was received with a sympathy due to his patriotic and fervid efforts, and to the cause in which he was engaged. A relief association was organized in Philadelphia, and considerable sums promptly contributed. A like reception awaited him in Boston. An opportunity was afforded him of addressing the legislature, and a resolution providing for an appropriation of a hundred thousand dollars from the State treasury was introduced. In aid of this movement, a public meeting of the citizens of Boston was called in Fanueil Hall, on the 10th February, 1864, of which the following account is extracted from the " Daily Advertiser " of the next day : —

"Fanueil Hall was crowded yesterday afternoon with a large audience called together by the announcement that Colonel Taylor, of East Tennessee, would make an address before the citizens of Boston, on the sufferings of the people of that region. A large number of ladies occupied seats in the gallery.

"About a quarter past four Colonel Taylor entered the hall, accompanied by His Excellency Governor Andrew, Hon. Edward Everett, Hon. J. E. Field, President of the Senate, Hon. A. H. Bullock, Speaker of the House, His Honor Mayor Lincoln, Collector Goodrich, Judge Thomas Russell, Hon. Robert C. Winthrop, Hon. C. G. Loring, Hon. J. Wiley Edmands, and several other distinguished gentlemen. Their entrance was the signal for enthusiastic applause by the audience.

"Honorable J. Wiley Edmands called the meeting to order, and said that the committee, appointed for the purpose of considering the best method of aiding the people of East Tennessee, had called this meeting so that the citizens of Boston might have an opportunity of hearing about their brethren in that region. Mr. Edmands stated that the committee had prepared the following list to be nominated as officers for the meeting, and they were, on motion, elected.

"*President,* — Hon. Edward Everett.

"*Vice-Presidents,* — His Excellency Governor Andrew, His Honor Mayor Lincoln, Hon. J. E. Field, Hon. A. H. Bullock, Hon. Robert C. Winthrop, Hon. Charles G. Loring, William Clafflin, Esq., Patrick Donahoe, Esq., William B. Rogers, Esq., Charles B. Goodrich, Esq., James Lawrence, Esq., Richard Frothingham, Esq., Julius Rockwell, Esq., Charles L. Woodbury, Esq., John M. Forbes, Esq.

"*Secretaries,* — Colonel F. L. Lee, and Samuel Frothingham, Jr.

"Honorable Edward Everett then stepped upon the platform, and spoke as follows" : —

SPEECH OF MR. EVERETT.

Fellow-Citizens : — We have come together for the grateful purpose of tendering a most cordial welcome to our honored guest, Colonel N. G. Taylor, of East Tennessee, and the pleasing duty has devolved upon me of introducing him to the Union-loving men of Boston, assembled in Faneuil Hall. I bid him a hearty welcome in your name. To introduce him, however, is wholly superfluous. Many of you have already heard him, and, as a matter of course, you desire to hear him again; all of you have heard of him, and, as a matter of course, you wish to hear from him. It is therefore as unnecessary, as it would be unbecoming in his presence, to dwell upon his titles to your respectful attention; but in addition to all his personal claims upon our sympathy, you will "hear him for his cause;" the cause, not simply of the Union, to which we are all devoted, but of faithful Union men, who, from the outbreak of the Rebellion, have stood at the post of danger; on whom the storm of war first broke; and on whom, from that day to this, it has beat with its wildest fury. At this distance from the seat of war, we hear only the far-off roar of the tempest; but all its waves and billows have gone over the devoted region, for which our honored guest comes to plead.

And a more interesting region, or one better entitled to our most active sympathy, is not to be found within the limits of the United States. Forming a part of the noble State of Tennessee, it is, in many respects, a

State of itself, and not a small one either. It consists
of the broad valley of the magnificent river, which
traverses it from northeast to southwest, three hundred miles in length, and with a varying width of
from fifty to seventy-five miles, — and of the slopes of
the mountains, which separate it on the north from
Kentucky, on the southwest from Middle Tennessee,
and on the southeast from North Carolina and Georgia: — a beautiful valley, between beautiful enclosing
hills, fertile many of them to their summits; sparkling
with a hundred tributaries to the noble stream which
forms its principal feature.

That river, fellow-citizens, is in some respects one of
the most remarkable on the continent. Its northern
affluents rise in the State of Virginia, but, as if to read
a lesson of patriotism in the very face of the soil, as if
to prop the fabric of the Union by the eternal but-
tresses of the hills, instead of flowing to the Atlantic
like the other rivers of Virginia, it gathers up the
waters of its tributary streams, Holston and Clinch and
French Broad, and connecting Virginia and the Caro-
linas with East Tennessee, flows southward down to the
northwestern corner of Georgia. There, after kissing
the feet of the glorious hills of Chattanooga, instead of
flowing to the Gulf, its seeming natural direction, it
coquets with Northern Alabama, breaks into the Mus-
cle Shoals, plants Decatur at their head, and Florence
at their feet, and then sweeping back to its native
North, traverses the entire width of Tennessee a second
time, apparently running up hill, — for while it is flowing northward, the Mississippi, parallel to it, and at no

great distance, is rolling its floods southward, — enters
the State of Kentucky, and empties at last into the
Ohio, fifty miles above the junction of that river with
the Mississippi, thus binding seven States in its silver
circuit, and connecting them all with the great central basin of the continent. The soil of Eastern Tennessee is rich, the mountains are filled with coal and
almost every variety of ore ; their slopes bubble with
mineral springs; the climate is temperate and healthful ; the territory divided into farms of a moderate
size, for the most part tilled by frugal, industrious men,
who own the soil, which yields them its well-earned
abundance. In no part of the State are there so few
slaves ; in none is there a more substantial population ; in no part of the South is the slave-interest so
feeble. East Tennessee greatly resembles the lower
ranges and fertile valleys of the Alps, and it has been
often called the American Switzerland. It is divided
into thirty counties, and its population does not, I
think, fall short of 300,000 souls. My friend, Colonel
Taylor, nods assent.

But this grand valley, with the hills that enclose it,
possesses an interest for us far beyond that which
attaches to their geographical features, merely as such.
It is one of the most important links in that chain of
valley and mountain, which traverses the entire North
American continent, from northeast to southwest, sep-
arating the streams which flow into the Atlantic from
those which seek the St. Lawrence, the Ohio, and the
Mississippi. Forcing its way down into the heart of the
region, whose alluvial plains are devoted to the culture

of tobacco, cotton, rice and sugar, by slave labor, this
ridge of highlands, with the valleys embosomed in them,
from the time you leave the State of Pennsylvania,
begins to assume the highest political importance, in
reference to the present stupendous struggle. Extend-
ing to the southwest as far as Northern Alabama, this
noble mountain tract, and the valleys enclosed in its
parallel and transverse ridges, is, by the character of
its climate, soil, and natural productions, the natural
ally of the North. Here, if nowhere else, we may truly
say, with the German poet —

> " Auf den Bergen ist Freiheit ; der Hauch der Grüfte
> Steigt nicht hinauf, in die reinen Lüfte."

That means —

> On the mountains is Freedom ; the breath of the vales
> Rises not up to the pure mountain gales.

Overrun it may be by the armed forces of the Rebellion, but all the sympathies and attachments of this
region are with the loyal States. While the aristoc-
racy of the southeastern counties of that State were
shouting " My Maryland," the farmers of the western
counties in Cumberland Valley, shouted back "No, it's
our Maryland." Western Virginia, a portion of the
same grand chain of mountain and valley, is as loyal
as Massachusetts. Then comes Western North Carolina, and still more Eastern Tennessee, the home of
our honored guest, and of as true hearted, loyal, Union-
loving a population as there is on the continent. As
far down as Northern Alabama the mountain district is

filled with Union sentiment. It was with the greatest difficulty that it was engineered into secession. As to East Tennessee, when an election was ordered by the disloyal Governor of Tennessee in that dark winter of February, 1861, to see if the State was willing to hold a convention for the purpose of seceding, there were 7,500 votes for the convention and 34,000 (nearly five to one) against it. This circumstance, when the treason of the cotton-growing States was consummated, marked out East Tennessee for the peculiar vengeance of the leaders of the rebellion. I will not anticipate what will be so much better stated by our honored guest; it is enough to say, that in addition to all the sufferings of regular warfare, the Union-loving inhabitants of East Tennessee have been the victims of lawless outrages and cruelties, of which the narrative curdles the blood.

Leaving all further detail to him, I will only recall to your recollection the letter of Mr. Judah P. Benjamin, at that time the rebel Secretary of War, of the 25th November, 1861. It will be remembered that, at this period of the war, the Government had been unable to send any aid to the loyal men of East Tennessee. It was before the glorious days of Grant at Chattanooga, and Burnside at Knoxville. Thrown upon their own resources, they naturally sought to save themselves from being overrun, by destroying the bridges on the chief lines of communication. One would suppose that, under the usurped rule of men, who professed to go to war for self-government and State-rights, the people of Eastern Tennessee, if for any reason they thought fit to do so, had a right to burn their own

2

bridges, without asking leave of the rebel cabal at
Richmond. But Mr. Jefferson Davis, a Mississippi
planter, and Mr. J. P. Benjamin, a lawyer of New Orleans, thought otherwise. They not only denied the
right of the farmers of East Tennessee to burn their
own bridges, but they undertook to outlaw the great
majority of the population of that region, five to one
faithful Union men, denouncing them as traitors, because they refused to commit treason. To show you
how the friends and neighbors of our honored guest
have been treated, let me read you that letter of the
New Orleans lawyer, who was under oath himself to
support the Constitution of the United States : —

" WAR DEPARTMENT, RICHMOND, Nov. 25, 1861.

" *Col. W. B. Wood:* Sir, — Your report of the 20th instant is
received, and I now proceed to give you the desired instruction in
relation to the prisoners of war taken by you among the *traitors*
of East Tennessee.

" First. All such as can be identified in having been engaged in
bridge-burning are to be tried summarily by *drum-head court-martial,*
and, if found guilty, *executed on the spot by hanging. It would
be well to leave their bodies hanging in the vicinity of the burned
bridges.*

" Second. All such as have not been so engaged are to be treated
as prisoners of war, and sent, with an armed guard, to Tuscaloosa,
Alabama, there to be kept imprisoned at the depot selected by the
Government for prisoners of war.

" Wherever you can discover that arms are concentrated by these
traitors, you will send out detachments, search for and seize the arms.
*In no case is one of the men known to have been up in arms against
the Government to be released on any pledge or oath of allegiance.*
The time for such measures is past. They are all to be treated as
prisoners of war, AND HELD IN JAIL TILL THE END OF THE WAR.

Such as come in voluntarily, take the oath of allegiance, and surrender their arms, are sure to be treated with leniency.

"Your vigilant execution of these orders is earnestly urged by the Government.

"Your obedient Servant,

"J. P. BENJAMIN, Secretary of War.

"COL. W. B. WOOD, Knoxville, Tenn.

"P. S. Judge Patterson, [Gov. Johnson's son-in-law,] Colonel Pickens, and other ringleaders of the same class, must be sent at once to Tuscaloosa to jail as prisoners of war."

Such was the atrocious letter of the rebel Secretary of War; such the treatment to which the Union men of East Tennessee have been subjected.

But I am encroaching on the time that belongs to our honored guest. I will only add, fellow-citizens, that our brethren of East Tennessee are fighting our battles as well as their own, on their blood-stained soil. It is our cause as much as theirs in which they have suffered the most cruel persecution; and however largely, however promptly, your relief may be extended to them, it will come too late, I fear, to rescue some of them from the horrors of starvation. This must not be. If the Union means anything, it means not merely political connection and commercial intercourse; but to bear each other's burdens and to share each other's sacrifices; it means active sympathy and efficient aid.

Colonel Taylor, on being introduced, was received with loud applause and hearty cheers. He addressed the assembly as follows:—

SPEECH OF COLONEL TAYLOR.

Mr. Chairman, Ladies, Gentlemen, Fellow-Citizens:—It is with feelings inexpressible that I appear before you to-day. It is with a gratification that I cannot find words to express, that I see so many of Boston's fair daughters and Boston's brave men. I am gratified, sir, at this assemblage and this presence, the more, when I remember that this assembly is convened, and that I am here to address it, not in my own behalf, but in behalf of my country, in behalf of my people in the mountains of East Tennessee; and I accept the presence of this assemblage, and the compliment thus offered, as an offering to my people of East Tennessee; for which, in their name, permit me, fellow-citizens, ladies, and gentlemen, to return you my grateful acknowledgments.

I regret that I cannot come here to tell you that we of East Tennessee are happy; that I cannot come here and tell you that our people are now as prosperous as they were wont to be; that in their quiet and peaceful vales at the base of their mountains, they are pursuing the avocations of domestic life, in the enjoyment of all that the Constitution of the United States guarantees to all its citizens. I regret that I cannot tell you to-day, fellow-citizens of Boston, that this is the condition of my country; but it is not my happiness to give you this sort of information. There is one thing, however, that it renders me happy to be able to tell you, and that is, though not blessed with the wealth that crowns you to-day, though not blessed with the prosperity that smiles all around upon your happy community, they have a heart that has ever, and still constantly and devotedly and passionately, in every circumstance and condition and trial of life, beats true to the flag of our country and the Union of these States.

My distinguished friend who has just addressed you has rendered it unnecessary for me, even if I could, to give you a description, geographically, of the country which I represent before you to-day; for he has painted it with the pencil of an artist, as he is, in word-painting, unexcelled within the limits of our broad country. While he has drawn the outline of that beautiful, and lovely, and loyal land, he has impressed his pictures with the warmth, and beauty, and patriotism of his own devoted heart. I come to you to-day, fellow-citizens, as the representative of East Tennessee, not to talk to you about party politics, not to make arguments or appeals for the support or the advancement of the interests of any particular party or any particular man in these United States; for I tell you, in all candor and truth, that such has been our condition, for more than two years, that we have had no party politics, as we used to understand them. It is true we have parties there, but there are only two. We once had a Democratic party, a Whig party, an American party, and an anti-American party; but these parties have all been merged in the great questions that have divided us for the last four years, — I might say, for the last eight years, and we are divided into only two parties: the one known as the Union party, and the other as the Secession or Rebel party; and I am glad to tell you to-day, as my illustrious friend has told you in advance, that when the test was applied at the ballot-box, we stood, in the thirty counties of East Tennessee, as thirty-four thousand to seven upon this question; thirty-four for the preservation of the Union of these States, and seven for the dissolution of this Government.

Neither do I come before you to-day, fellow-citizens, as a beggar, although I present myself somewhat in the semblance of one; nor do I represent a begging, although a 'beggared people. She whose people were too proud to bow the neck and receive the yoke of King Cotton of the South, is too proud at heart to ask alms at the hands of her sisters of the North. But I come, as the representative of a suffering and loyal people, reduced to extremity by reason of their devotion to our common country, to present some plain facts to the loyal people of the North and of the West, that they may have an opportunity for the extension of that benevolence, which opens its hand always to the suffering and the faithful everywhere.

It is true, fellow-citizens, that many of our kindred of the South are very angry with the people of East Tennessee, and they hate us with great bitterness, and of late have done us great injury. Yet, while the remembrance of this fact is a source of great pain to the people of East Tennessee, they are consoled by the reflection that this animosity and hatred have been engendered by her devotion to the union of these States, by her adherence to the farewell advice of our glorious Washington, the Father of our country; by her persistent refusal to take part or lot in any mad effort for the overthrow of our common Government, — a Government which has always protected its citizens, which has never infringed a solitary right of an individual or a State of this Union, from its beginning down, and which our people believe it to be their religious duty to hand down, as a priceless and inestimable heritage, to their children and children's children.

But, fellow-citizens, it is not true that East Tennessee has ever been unfaithful to the Southern people, either in principle or in fact. We believed, and we declared, that the interests and institutions, the happiness, prosperity, and rights of the people of the South were bound up with and in the Union, and that they could never be preserved outside of the Union. We declared this upon the rostrum, and at the hustings, everywhere, from Carter to Shelby, — from the eastern limit of the State to its western boundary upon the Mississippi River. History has been written, fellow-citizens, and its immutable verdict is, that our judgment was right and correct, and it has demonstrated that their's was false and fallacious. Let the universal prosperity that swelled every channel of our vitality — commercial, political, industrial, and social — at the beginning of the war, and within the Union, attest this fact; and let their ruined commerce, their paralyzed industry, their bankrupt treasury, the dismembered families, the brokenhearted widows, the orphaned children, the desolated homes and new-made graves, without the Union, attest the unutterable folly of those who execrated the people of East Tennessee because they would not affiliate with treason. Could those who made this war be made alone to taste its bitterness and feel its woes, it had been well indeed. Then East Tennessee would have escaped. But, alas! the concentrated fury of the war has rolled over her innocent bosom, and she is in ruins to-day, having nothing left her but pride, poverty, and patriotism. Her people are the descendants of the pioneer heroes of North Carolina, Virginia, Maryland, Pennsylvania, and New Jersey, with here and there an individual from other Northern and Southern States of the United States; and, like their illustrious ancestry, they have never learned how to prove false to the Constitution and Union of the country. The pioneer heroes of East Tennessee left their daughters, their wives and their old men, to defend their homes against a savage foe, in the great war for Independence, while they buckled on their armor, and struck upon the sides of King's Mountain, under the lead of Shelby and Campbell, for our infant nationality. In the war of 1812, they fought gallantly on many a battle-field, and triumphed under the immortal Jackson at New Orleans. In 1832–33, when Nullification threatened with the sword to cut the gordian knot of our beloved Union, and when the illustrious Jackson appealed to the Eternal to witness that the Federal Union must be preserved, a united Amen swelled in the hearts and broke from the lips of the people of East Tennessee, as from the lips of one man, and they were ready to sacrifice their lives in defence of the integrity of our glorious Government. Her stalwart sons were mingled in the front ranks of the Mexican war, and they poured out their blood freely with their fellow-citizens of other States at Vera Cruz and Cerro Gordo, at Monterey and

Buena Vista, at Chepultepec and Cherubusco, and helped to swell the shout of victory as our gallant legions marched in triumph into the Grand Plaza of Mexico.

Thus, fellow-citizens, in peace and in war, in the cabinet and in the field, at the hustings, at the bar, and in the Senate, in public assemblies and private circles, in the homes of the rich and the cabins of the poor, the heart of East Tennessee beats time to the music of the Union. Witness the sad history of the past three years! This devotion is not a mere sentiment, it is a passion; nay, more, it is a principle on fire, ever burning, never consumed; it is a heritage of the blood, transmitted from sire to son, imbibed with mother's milk; stereotyped upon the heart, and riveted in the soul.

The first test of the Union sentiment of East Tennessee, in reference to the existing difficulties, was applied, as has been remarked by my friend, the Chairman of the meeting, in February, 1861. The form of the question then was, A Convention or No Convention, and representatives or delegates to be elected by the people to that Convention, in case it should receive a majority in its favor at the pending election? The true test in this election was the aggregate majority of those who vindicated the Union cause during the contest. The questions before the people were amply discussed from the rostrum, and when the day for election came, the State of Tennessee, casting a vote of 130,000 or 140,000, gave a solid majority of 64,000 opposed to going out of the Union of these States; and of that number, fellow-citizens, East Tennessee gave 34,000 in favor of the Union, and 7,000 against it. In June,

when the question was put in a different form —
Representation or No Representation? — East Tennessee again recorded her vote, by overwhelming majorities, against the great treason. Then came persuasions, soft and sweet, and silent eloquence dropped like the dews of Hermon into the ears of our people of the mountains, and our young men were promised exemption from the battle-field if they would only acquiesce and let the storm roll on. Well, fellow-citizens, the August election came, and the question was to elect a Governor, members of Congress, and representatives to the State Legislature. By that time, the bristling bayonets of the Southern Confederacy were found all over the State of Tennessee. Our great men in the middle and western portions of the State had felt the force of the storm; among them, the man whom I was proud to follow, in 1860, as the representative of the Union sentiment of our State, in conjunction with my illustrious friend on my right — I mean, fellow-citizens, John Bell. He, and the Ewings, Cave Johnson, Neal Brown, and a host of men whose hearts had been true to the Union until the storm rose, now felt their knees smite together and their hearts fail them, and the fury of the tempest swept them all off into the Southern Confederacy. Our boys in the mountains saw the gathering storm. Efforts were made to keep us from the ballot-box. We were told — "The State having now gone out of the Union, if you dare to go and vote for the men who are in favor of the old Union, we will see that you are taken care of. We have places prepared for men of your sentiments, and the first thing you

know you will find yourselves under the gallows, or in the loathsome dungeons of the Southern Confederacy." The storm came up, from the west and south, and the east of us, — dark, gloomy, gathering blackness with every hour. We heard the muttering thunders in its bosom, we saw the livid flashes, as they flashed upon us in our isolated position. But, fellow-citizens, when the election came, when the rest of the State was falling off and going into treason and the Southern Confederacy, East Tennessee, as far as she was concerned, elected her candidate for Governor, her representatives to the Congress of the United States, and her representatives to the legislature, by overwhelming majorities. It was all sorts of an election. We had candidates for various offices in the Confederacy, and candidates for the same offices in the Union; and in my District, the candidate for the Congress of the United States was elected to that Congress, and he was also elected to the Congress of the Confederate States.

Then came, my friends, the violence to individuals; then came the cutting down and shooting down of Union flags; but still, East Tennessee breasted the storm, she still held out faithful; and by and by the Confederate Congress, when the war waxed hot and hotter, passed a conscript law, and every man in the community, from eighteen to thirty-five years of age, was enrolled by officers in every neighborhood, appointed for that purpose, and notified to rally at a given time and at a given point, to enter active service for the defence of the rebel cause. Then the exodus, already begun, swelled to hundreds and thousands. Our young men had resolved that they never, — no, *never*, — could be persuaded or charmed by blandishments or flattery, or forced by bayonets, to strike at the heart of the mother that bore them. No, fellow-citizens, but they went to their homes, kissed their mothers' lips and received their blessing; they received the fond farewells of their fathers, their sisters, their wives and their little ones, and then went forth exiles from their own loved land, and for no other reason than that they loved that land. There was no promise of premiums or bounties to them; there was no hope of wealth, happiness, and prosperity in the distance; but they left their homes in the darkness of the night, and ascended the rocky sides of the mountains, one hundred and fifty or two hundred miles from Kentucky, where they hoped to find relief. Ragged and in tatters, with their feet unshod and bleeding, they took the pathless ridges of the mountains, in the darkness of the night, aided by the silvery rays of the moon or the dimmer light of the stars; and, in the daytime, sought the deepest, darkest gorges of the mountains, that they might find shelter and rest until the coming shadows of another night enabled them again to pursue their perilous way, that they might find liberty and the flag of their country, under its folds alone to fight, and, if need be, there to die.

Regiments, companies, and squads of infantry and cavalry were now distributed over the length and breadth of the country, for the purpose of hunting down and shooting the escaping conscripts. Everywhere they went, fellow-citizens; and as they went they entered the houses of the people, searching for arms and ammunition, and thus the people of the whole county were robbed of their muskets and rifles, and left perfectly defenceless. Prominent citizens were arrested now, by armed bands, frequently at midnight, in the bosom of their families, without notice, and carried before some provost marshal, or some upstart official, tried before a military commission, hastily got together, *ex parte*, without evidence, and with scarcely the semblance of a charge, sometimes with no charge at all, and then hurried off to the loathsome dungeons of Tuscaloosa, Ala., or Madison, Ga., or Richmond, or Salisbury, or Knoxville, or Nashville, there to lie in the midst of unutterable filth and vermin, to pine away and famish upon their scanty and miserable fare, and sometimes to die in utter despair. I, myself, have known the facts of which I speak. Men as reputable as any in East Tennessee have suffered in this way. I will mention one case. Mr. Pickens, (whose name is mentioned in the letter of the Confederate Secretary of State, which has been read by my friend, the Chairman,) had been a representative in the State Legislature. He was a man of heart, a man of soul, a man of intelligence, a man who was popular among all our people, a good citizen, and true and loyal to his country; but he had been ostracized, and in compliance with the order of which I find a copy in the hands of my friend, he was seized, without charges, carried South, and in the loathsome dungeons of Tuscaloosa, Ala., he paid the forfeit of his life, and became a martyr to the glorious cause of human liberty and the Union of these States.

Sir, such instances are not rare in our community. The prisons of the South have been filled with the best men of East Tennessee; and it is said by those who know, that not less than five thousand — think of it, fellow-citizens! — not less than five thousand of the men of East Tennessee, because they were true to their country, because they loved the flag that emblematized all that they held dearest on earth, because they would not bow the knee to Baal, nor receive upon their necks the yoke of the king of the South, have been snatched from their homes by the hand of lawless power, and borne away into captivity. The railroad bridge near where I lived was burned, and the parties charged with burning it were arrested, tried by a drum-head court-martial, according to the order which you have heard read, and hung; and, fellow-citizens, I speak the truth when I tell you, that at least two of those gentlemen — for they were gentlemen, honorable, high-minded, intelligent, moral, upright citizens of the community in which they lived — two, at least, I say, of those who were thus ignominiously hung, and their bodies left dangling in the air, knew not that they were sentenced until they were brought within sight of the gibbet upon which they were to expiate with their lives that offence which they had committed against the Southern Confederacy, — of being true to their own Government!

Thus affairs moved on, fellow-citizens, and Terror planted her black flag over all our country; and, to make the reign of Terror still more fearful, a legion of tawny Indians, whose forefathers had been wont, in

earlier times, to tomahawk and scalp the citizens of
our section of the country, were brought from their
mountain regions, with their painted faces and wild,
unearthly whoops, and put upon the track of our remaining young men. But be it ever remembered, to
their credit, that these poor, half-civilized Cherokees
were less savage on the trail than their pale-faced com-
panions in arms ; and the people of my section of country, after the first terror had subsided, and they found
the kindness of heart that existed in the bosoms of
these people, preferred a thousand Cherokee Indians
among their homes to one captain's company of rebel
Southern soldiers.

Several regiments of citizens had now volunteered,
and hundreds more had been compelled by coercion
to enter the rebel lines, and to serve in the rebel
army ; and about this time, August, 1863, Jeff. Davis
made another call, running up to forty-five years of
age ; and at the same time, Governor Harris issued an
additional call, embracing all up to fifty-five years of
age ; so you see that all our population from eighteen
years of age up to fifty-five were called for by these
several authorities. But simultaneously with these calls
came the advance of General Burnside's gallant and
glorious army across the Cumberland Mountains, for the
redemption and relief of our suffering people. The
army of General Bragg had been, just previous, compelled to evacuate Chattanooga, and thus General Rose-
crans occupied that extremity of the State; and many of
our young men at once sprung from their hiding-places
and their coverts in the mountains, and rallied to the
standard of their country, under the lead of these gal-

lant and glorious champions of the Union, and our
mothers, sisters, wives, and old men were left alone
to occupy our vacant homes. To-day, fellow-citizens,
more than 25,000 Tennesseeans wear the uniform and
bear the arms of your country and my country.
[Prolonged and enthusiastic applause.] While I would
not disparage any other portion of these United States
in its patriotism and devotion to country, I must say
for my section, that in the midst of all the sufferings
and trials, privations and perils incident to every hour
of their lives, they have furnished to the support of
your Government and my Government more men, in
proportion to their population — more than two to
one — than any other part of our common country.

As General Burnside, in September, marched with
his conquering hosts towards Upper Tennessee, the
rebel army retreated before him; but as they went,
thinking, perhaps, that they were seeing the last of
East Tennessee, they seized upon the property, the
live stock, especially of the Union farmers, all over
the country, where they could find it, and carried
it off with them. From that moment, the work of
·devastation went on with accelerated momentum.
Four times have the Union and rebel armies trav-
ersed the whole length of East Tennessee, exhausting
the country all around for current supplies, and at
every movement, widening the track of ruin that they
left behind them. In the track of the armies came
robbers, who found convenient hiding-places and ral-
lying points in the mountains that skirt our valleys,
and came down and claimed their share of the property of our plundered people; and thus it came to

pass that our barns and stables, our cribs and dwell-ings, were entered and robbed, and our people left utterly destitute. The very wearing apparel of our women and children was seized by these ruffians and carried out of our houses. Our blankets and bed-clothing, everything of woollen that was calculated to render the soldiers more comfortable, was seized by the strong hand, and carried away. Our tanneries shared the same fate. They had all been compelled, in the reign of the rebels, to contribute sixty per cent. of their leather to the Government for the shoeing of their soldiers; but now, when they were retreating from the State, they seized all the leather in the vats and bore it away, leaving our old men and women and children to meet the rigors of the passing winter bare-footed, as well as almost naked.

Believe me, fellow-citizens, East Tennesse has drunk the full cup of suffering, and nothing seems left her now but to drain its bitterness to the very dregs. She has sacrificed everything but loyalty and honor; she has suffered everything but dishonor and death; and now destitution and famine, followed by despair and death, are trampling upon the thresholds of her sad homes, are entering their very doors, ready to con-summate the sacrifice and complete the suffering. But, thank God, throughout her sufferings she has been faithful. Persuasions, threats, insults, imprisonments, wounds, stripes, privations, chains, confiscations, gib-bets and military murders, the clash of arms, the terri-bleness of armies with banners, and all the combined and concentrated horrors of internecine war marshalled

3 *

upon her battle-torn bosom and hurling sorrow and ruin into all her homes, have never corrupted her loyalty, nor driven her a solitary line from her devotion to the Government of her fathers. Left unprotected, when she ought to have been protected by the Government that she loved, interior and isolated, disarmed before she could organize, she was choked down by tyranny, under a reign of terror black as the night of the Robesperian dynasty, and her proud neck felt the heel of a despotism more relentless and crushing than the power of an autocracy. Her loyal people, because they could not do otherwise, suffered the infliction of a bondage which their inmost hearts abhorred — a bondage that fettered the soul and sealed the lips, and all but closed the door of hope. We know, fellow-citizens, what history means when it tells us of a " Reign of Terror." Such a state of things is only to be felt ; it never can be told. It comes to me now, even here on the free soil of Massachusetts, not as a reality in the retrospect, but like the memory of some horrid dream, to disturb and haunt me along my pathway of life. God grant that I may never feel the iron heel of such a despotism in my soul again, nor see it in the bosom of my fellow-citizens anywhere ! We breathe but to live ; and live but to pray — " Oh, Lord, how long ? " But, thank God ! the prayer of the loyalist, leaping up from the heart, cannot be held by the hand of the oppressor, and East Tennessee, in answer to our prayers, is almost free, and the old banner waves once more triumphantly, gloriously, over our mountain-girt home, and there may it float forever !

With this history of the people of East Tennessee before you, fellow-citizens, it is for you to determine whether this brave and patriotic population shall be suffered to fall and perish in their devotion to our common country, by the blighting hand of famine, or whether your philanthropy and benevolence shall interpose to shield and protect and guard and save them. East Tennessee, my native East Tennessee, has sacrificed all she had for the country. Her horses, her mules, her flocks and herds, her cattle upon a thousand hills, have all been offered up ; her corn and wheat are all consumed ; her young men — all who have not perished in the camp or on the battle-field — are now swelling the ranks of your victorious armies ; and, sir, our matrons and maidens, our old men and little children, our soldiers' widows and orphaned babes, are all bound and upon the altar ; already the sacrificial knife is uplifted ; it trembles in the hand of Famine ; — may God save my people, and avert the stroke, in this their day of sorrow and trial !

While the scourges of this cruel war have thus blighted and blasted, devastated and ruined East Tennessee, the home of the free, the home of the loyal and the brave, they have scarcely been felt north of Mason and Dixon's line. On the contrary, a degree of prosperity, such as you have never before experienced, has poured into the lap of the people of the North and West boundless wealth. The labors of your agriculturists have been succeeded by the blessings of a gracious Providence ; your mechanics have received remunerative prices for all the labor they could perform ; your merchants have seen their trade prosper beyond all parallel; your manufacturers have extended and en-larged their operations in every branch of industry; and your mineral region is pouring forth, from the bounties of the earth, uncounted wealth. Whether you, fellow-citizens, will make this vast increase of wealth a source of blessing to yourselves, your children, your country and the world, is a problem that is left for you to solve. The desolations and ruin of this unnatural and cruel war have opened a wide field for your philanthropy and benevolence. Will you enter it? — will you sow it? — will you cultivate it? If so, an abundant crop of blessings will fall upon your basket and upon your store, upon your homes and hearths, and, above all, upon your hearts.

When starving Ireland was weeping over her famishing children, and as they were drooping and dying in the remorseless grasp of famine, her wail of woe was heard across the wide waste of waters, and America wept in sympathy with Ireland; but while she lifted up, with one hand, their dying heads, with the other she ministered nourishment and life to the perishing children of the Emerald Isle. A nobler example of national magnanimity and Christian charity can scarcely be produced from the annals of the world. Yet these people were the subjects of a foreign Government, and were strangers beyond the sea. The cry of suffering now comes to the American ear and falls upon the American heart from the famishing lips of our own people; and East Tennessee, from the summit of her róck-ribbed mountains, with one hand beckons to her rich and powerful and flourishing sisters of the North, and with a bursting heart and tearful eye points with the other to the desolation that hangs like a pall of death over her forty thousand ruined homes in the valleys below. Will those sisters prove again angels of blessing and angels of mercy to bring peace and happiness and hope to those desolate homes, or will they leave their past munificence alone to illustrate and glorify their future history? That you, fellow-citizens, do sympathize with my people, and that you are ready to open your hands for their relief, I cannot doubt; and especially when I remember that the appeal of the suffering and the sorrowful, the afflicted and the bereaved of earth has never been made in vain to your magnanimous legislature, nor to your magnanimous and benevolent people. Sir, the question is reduced to one of life or death. General Grant, as I learn from General Robert Anderson, wrote to him the other day, saying that there were three alternatives for the people of East Tennessee : one was, to be carried out of their section to where they could find something to eat; another was, that provisions should be carried to them; and the last was, if neither of the others was adopted, that the people of East Tennessee must perish in the midst of their mountains. Sir, I do not believe you intend that these people shall perish. I will not believe it till I see their bones bleaching among their native hills. I believe you have hearts that palpitate in unison with their hearts; I believe you have hands that will open for their relief.

Sir, we must be relieved from destitution ; but that

is not all we must be relieved from. We must be relieved from the weight of this crushing war. How is that to be accomplished? Somebody is to be subjugated. Either the traitors who have aimed at the life of this great nation must be conquered, or the remnants of the people who have bared their bosoms to the storm, who have seen their homes made desolate for their love of country, must feel again the heel of the traitor on their necks. Sir, this war must be ended; peace must come again; we cannot live in this state; it is abnormal; it is opposed to all our hopes and wishes. We all love peace and desire peace; but those traitors who would not have peace at the beginning are not ready now to embrace peace. A voice comes up from their homes, — a voice comes up from tens of thousands of new-made graves in the sunny South, — a voice comes up from an ocean of tears, spreading over the land, — a voice comes up from tens of thousands of acres of waving cotton-fields of the past, reminding them of the blessings of peace. Their prosperous homes, their broad fields, their widespread sails of commerce, their open ports, their accumulated wealth, their growing importance and grandeur, are all so many voices pleading for peace with that people; and yet they will not hear of peace. And, sir, that is not all. The very God of heaven says — Peace! Peace! Peace! But they will not hearken; they will not hearken to the voice that comes from the tombs of their dead; they will not hearken to the appeal of interest, that comes to them from every channel of commerce and industry through-

out their land ; they will not hearken to the cry of the
people that suffer here, nor to the warning that comes
from abroad, from those who love liberty, and pray
for peace. They have passed all this by, and now I
tell you there is only one way to obtain peace. And
what is that ? By crying peace to them ? — by talking moral suasion ? — No, sir, no ! I ask you, sir, can
we get peace, happy, lovely, glorious, lasting peace, by
quibbling over questions of constitutional law and
talking about violated rights, and the rights of traitors,
if they will come back into this Union, while they are
pointing their daggers at the very heart of our nationality itself? No, sir. The temple that contains the
treasures of a nation and the hopes of posterity in all
time to come is blazing ; the smoke is flying upward
as incense to heaven ; and what should you think of
the firemen who approached that temple to extinguish
the flames, and instead of sending the antagonistic
element to quell the fire, went to quarrelling as to
who should throw the water first ? Sir, the ship is in
danger ; on her port is Scylla, on her lee is Charybdis ;
behind her is a reef, and breakers are before her ; the
storm is spending its fury all around, and pirates
are on her track. Shall the crew of that noble vessel,
freighted with our wives and children and loved ones,
freighted with our hopes for all time to come, freighted
with the prospects of liberty and the hopes of freedom
of all earth's inhabitants that know or have heard of
us — shall her crew, in the midst of this storm, fall to
fighting as to who shall next command the ship ? Oh,
is it not the part of patriotism for every man, in this

dark hour, to come and strengthen the heart of the helmsman to stand at his post? [Enthusiastic and prolonged applause.] And no matter what questions may separate and divide that crew, is it not their duty to stand in the midst of the storm, and say to the helmsman — "Guide our bark safely through! Here we are, at your back, and we will stand by you through the storm!" [Renewed applause.] Sir, if we do this, the vessel will soon pass between Scylla and Charybdis, she will leap over the breakers and the reefs, and when we get out upon a calm sea, and upon a prosperous voyage, then, and not until then, can we settle the questions that we may choose to raise.

Sir, I have said that we want peace, and must have peace. But how shall we get it? There is but one way, that I know of. Let it gleam upon the bristling points of fifteen hundred thousand bayonets [tremendous and long-continued applause]; let it blaze upon the glittering steel of five hundred thousand swords; let it leap from the mouths of ten thousand cannon, and the echo of that thunder will bring peace to every home and house and heart throughout the length and breadth of our reunited country. When the atmosphere is damp and filled with malaria, and death moves in every breeze, then, sir, what do we want? We want the keen flash of heaven's electricity, we want the live thunder, rolling from mountain top to mountain top; and then all is purified, all is calm, all is serene and healthful once more.

Sir, I trust the time is coming, and will soon be here, when this cruel war will be over. I trust the

day is soon coming which is to prove but the dawn of
that prosperity which is in reservation for our glorious
country in the near and far-off future, when, reunited,
we shall sit under our own vine and fig-tree everywhere, and none shall make us afraid; when the voice
of the sentinels upon Liberty's watch-tower, as it is
uttered upon the coast of the Atlantic, shall be echoed
all along the line, until the last man hears and returns
the salutation from the shore of the far-off Pacific.

Sir, permit me, in conclusion, to say, in the language
of the illustrious statesman who now sleeps his last
sleep at Marshfield, "Liberty and Union, one and
inseparable, now and forever!" [Loud and prolonged
applause, and three hearty cheers for Colonel Taylor.]

At the conclusion of Colonel Taylor's remarks,
George B. Upton, Esq. offered the following resolutions, which were adopted unanimously by the meeting : —

"*Resolved*, That the warmest sympathy of all loyal and humane
Americans is due to the suffering Unionists of East Tennessee, for
the steadfast fidelity with which they have maintained the cause of
our common country in the midst of peril and distress, for the
spirit with which the men have rallied to defend the flag, for the
devotion with which the women and children have sacrificed their
diminished resources to feed our armies.

"*Resolved*, That patriotism, sound policy, and humanity alike require that the extreme need of these our brethren and sisters should
be relieved from the overflowing abundance with which Providence
has blessed us, even in time of civil war.

"*Resolved*, That we call upon our Legislature to make a liberal
grant in aid of the loyal population of East Tennessee, and that it will
be a matter of just pride that the name of our old Commonwealth
shall head the National subscription, which will carry hope and life
to those noble men and women."

4

On motion of Mr. Upton the officers of the meeting were appointed a Committee to present the subject of the resolutions to the Legislature.

Repeated calls were made for Governor Andrew, and, at the request of the Governor, Mr. Everett announced that the state of His Excellency's health was such that he was compelled to ask the meeting to excuse him from making any remarks.

Honorable Robert C. Winthrop ascended the platform in response to repeated calls. He excused himself from speaking at length. He said that from first to last in this terrible strife his heart had been with the Border States. He had felt that the Border States had been the hinge of the whole contest. With them he had been willing to go wherever they led, and to stop whenever they felt obliged to stop, whether upon subjects relating to slavery or the Constitution. He had felt that with them we might save this Government, without them we must inevitably lose it. He trusted that nothing would be left undone for relieving the sufferings, and encouraging and rewarding the loyalty, of the people of the Border States, and particlarly of East Tennessee, whether by individual contribution or legislative appropriation.

REMARKS BY JUDGE RUSSELL.

Judge Russell being called out by the audience, spoke substantially as follows : —

Fellow-Citizens : — I hope "I dare do all that may become" a very modest young man, but I dare not

address an audience that has been thrilled by eloquence such as we have heard to-day. It has seemed
to me that we listened, not to Colonel Taylor's voice
alone, but to the voice of Eastern Tennessee herself, —
her loyalty, her fidelity, the courage of her men, the
patriotism, the suffering, the agony of her women and
her children. Colonel Taylor needs no indorsement,
but we know that he has for every word the full indorsement of the noble Burnside. Let me add, that
this testimony is confirmed by one of the Generals who
marched to relieve Burnside. General Blair has just
told me a touching story of the devotion of the women
who crowded to the line of his forced march to welcome the sight of our armies; to wave the flags which
in evil days they had hidden in the secret recesses
of their homes, even as they kept the love of Union
in their hearts; to bring the last piece of bacon, the
last handful of meal, to feed the advancing soldiers of
the Union cause. Often, he said, he forbade his men
to take the scanty gifts of the poor. As often, he
heard the reply: "Take it; I have a husband, a son
at Knoxville; take it all for the Union." These are
the people for whom our aid is sought.

A friend has just asked whether it is in the power
of the Legislature to make the proposed grant. I am
glad no one doubts that it is in their hearts. I know
nothing in our State Constitution which forbids an act
of humanity and patriotism. It is for the "support
and defence of Government" to guard the outposts in
Tennessee; it is for the "preservation" of the people
here to preserve the loyal people there. Nor are prec-

edents wanting, if precedents are needed for an act of generosity and of justice. Soon after the adoption of our Constitution, the State passed a resolve, and incurred expense to aid the suffering inhabitants of South Carolina. God hasten the day when the relations of South Carolina and Massachusetts shall again be such that the cry of distress there shall meet a ready answer in our own Commonwealth. We have made a State grant to help build a monument to Washington, in the capital. Can we vote supplies to honor the memory even of the greatest among our deceased patriots, and is it unconstitutional to keep alive the families of those patriots who stand in arms for the flag? We have helped to raise another monument to the signers of the Declaration. Can we do nothing to support that people whose position, whose very existence to-day, is the proudest testimonial to the love of Union, and the strongest assurance that the Union shall be eternal? I do not fear the legal question. I am only anxious that what is done shall be done at once. Our friend has spoken of America's gifts to Ireland, gifts so well repaid by the devotion of Ireland's sons in the day of our country's trial. Let me once more recall to your minds the words of Mr. Everett, when he pleaded in Fanueil Hall for the famine-stricken Irish. "Even now," he said in closing that appeal, "even now, while I have filled your ears with empty words, some of our fellow-Christians have starved to death." And now, while we are preparing to seek our comfortable homes, some of our fellow-patriots are sinking in despair. "Want, like an armed man," stalks among the desolated homes of Eastern Tennessee. Famine hardly delays to strike, and pestilence, sure attendant of famine, glooms in the horizon. God help those faithful hearts; and may He so move our hearts that our hands may be open and our feet be swift to bear deliverance to those of our brethren who are almost ready to perish.

The following letter from General Frank Blair was then read : —

"BOSTON, *February* 9, 1864.

"*Honorable· J. Wiley Edmands:* Dear Sir, — I have received your invitation to address a meeting to be held in behalf of the loyal people of East Tennessee, at Faneuil Hall, on Wednesday evening next. I regret that my engagements will not permit me to attend. It has been my fortune recently to pass through that country, and to witness the suffering and distress which have been inflicted upon that people on account of their steadfast and devoted loyalty to their country. No people have been more faithful and none have had their faith so tried. After the battle of Chattanooga I marched in command of the 15th Army Corps, under General Sherman, to the relief of Burnside at Knoxville. We passed through a country which had already been visited by both hostile armies, and pillaged with unrelenting cruelty by the rebels on account of the loyalty of the people. Our troops were without rations or supplies of any kind, having been ordered to give up the pursuit of Bragg's flying army and march to the relief of Knoxville without an opportunity of obtaining anything of the kind, and were compelled to forage on the country. The people on our approach came out to meet us, bringing with them their scant supplies, and freely offered them to our soldiers. They cheered us with kind words, and waved the old flag, which they had cherished in secret, and implored us to hasten to the succor of their kindred, who composed a part of the garrison of Knoxville.

"I trust that the people of Massachusetts will hearken to the appeal of Colonel Taylor, and that their liberality, so well known and so often felt in the remotest quarters of our country, will be stimulated by the remembrance of the kindness and devotion of the loyal women of Tennessee who succored our toil-worn soldiers on their march to the relief of their beleaguered brothers, many of whom were sons of Massachusetts.

"I am, with great respect, your obedient servant,

"FRANK P. BLAIR."

The foregoing proceedings, as has been stated, appeared in the Boston journals of the next day, the 11th February. It will be observed that the only measure of relief contemplated by the Resolutions was an appropriation from the treasury of the Commonwealth. The Committee appointed had reference to that object, and no arrangement was made for individual subscriptions, it having been doubtless considered that an energetic movement for that purpose might be regarded by members of the two houses, as superseding the necessity of legislative action.

But though no provision was made for receiving private subscriptions, a chord had been touched by Colonel Taylor, which drew a sympathetic response from the heart of the community. On the same day on which it was written I received the following letter, apparently in a female hand, enclosing three dollars:—

"BOSTON, 11 *February*, 1864.

"*Dear Sir:* — Enclosed is a ' mite' which I wish forwarded with the thousands and tens of thousands of dollars that I hope will be sent forward from this goodly city of Boston, to alleviate the unparalleled sufferings of our dearly beloved countrymen in East Tennessee.

"Such earnest, eloquent pleading as comes to us from our old ' cradle of liberty' cannot be unheeded by any patriot or lover of his race.

"TEACHER OF A PUBLIC SCHOOL.

"MR. EVERETT."

Having no other means of acknowledging this anonymous letter, I sent it for publication, the next day, to the Editor of the "Daily Advertiser," with the following note : —

"The accompanying letter was received by me to-day, with a three dollar bill enclosed. I request its publication, not merely on account of the pure spirit of patriotic and Christian charity which it discloses, but in the hope that it may serve as an example to others. Small as the sum is, I doubt not it is large for the means of the giver, and it will sustain the life of one of our starving brethren in East Tennessee for a fortnight. If a small portion only of our community would, according to their ability, imitate this example, that desolated region might again become ' the happy valley ' of the South."

On the same day on which this note appeared in the " Daily Advertiser " (12th February), a letter was addressed to me by Mr. F. H. Peabody, of the banking-house of J. E. Thayer & Company, enclosing a check for one hundred dollars, which was accompanied by a donation of fifty dollars from his brother, Lieut.-Colonel Peabody. In the hope of obtaining their consent to mention their names, these liberal donations were not announced on the 13th. To my great regret, these young gentlemen insisted that their generous contributions should be announced anonymously. It is only for the purpose of this publication that they have yielded to my request that their names should now be mentioned. I also received on the 12th an anonymous line from a " Boston Boy," enclosing five dollars as " another mite for the sufferers in East Tennessee."

The announcement of this donation in the "Daily Advertiser " of the 13th was accompanied with the following remarks : —

"In making this second announcement, I would express the hope that the movements of public and private liberality will not interfere with each other. One friend has said to me, with reference to the proposed legislative appropriation, that the sympathy of individuals was the proper dependence in cases of this kind; while another friend has suggested that the aggregate of suffering to be relieved is too vast for anything but the public resources. This last view, I fear, is nearer the truth, or rather the suffering is so general and so extreme, that after public and private liberality have both done their best, much want will remain hopelessly unrelieved. In addition to the cruel outrages inflicted upon the loyal people of East Tennessee, for the two long years that the Government was unable to extend to them any military protection, — outrages of which so shocking a picture was presented by Colonel Taylor, — this devoted region has latterly been the battle-field of two large, hostile armies, operating far from their chief base of supplies. It is now utterly exhausted. The rich, the people in moderate circumstances, and the poor have been brought down to one common ghastly level of destitution, and are in want of food and clothing. It is plain that nothing but ample appropriations from the large and prosperous States can effectually face this great amount of suffering, and that there will still be enough of want left to require all the aid that can be derived from private liberality."

On Monday, the 15th, the donations of the Messrs. Peabody were announced, with an extract of the letter of Mr. F. H. Peabody, in which he says, "The behavior of the people of East Tennessee is something that every American will be proud of for ages to come. Now that Colonel Taylor has told us how to be useful in the matter, I believe the people of Massachusetts will give very substantial proof of their admiration for the most splendid patriotism of the age." A donation of five dollars from a lady in Yarmouth Port, transmitted in a letter of the 13th, expressive of "warm sympathy for the suffering East Tennesseeans" was acknowledged also on the 15th.

Such was the commencement of the movement for the three days which followed the meeting in Fanueil Hall. I have thought it a matter of interest to narrate it with some particularity. The daily record of donations announced at the time and now reproduced for preservation will show the steady and rapid growth of the fund. Liberal contributions steadily flowed in, anonymously in many cases, although at my earnest request, publicly expressed, and privately addressed to donors when known to me, they sometimes consented to the mention of their names. Letters of approval and encouragement were also addressed to me by persons of influence. Among the earliest of these (15th February) was C. P. Curtis, Esq., who accompanied his liberal donation with the request that it should " be remitted to the cruelly used people of East Tennessee." On the same day, W. H. Gardiner, Esq., addressed a letter to me, in which he remarked that " of· the almost innumerable calls for aid caused by this grievous war, I know none, after the care of our own soldiers, so unexceptionable or making so strong an appeal to all who have anything to give, as that of the loyal Tennesseeans. Yet we are moving very slowly. Private citizens seem to be waiting for some action of the Legislature. The Legislature seems to be waiting to know how the people would like to see their money given away ; but while we ponder, East Tennessee starves." This letter enclosed the generous donation of two hundred dollars.

Thus far, I had acted wholly as a volunteer in receiving and announcing donations, but evidently the time had arrived for some organized movement. A meeting was accordingly held at my house on the 17th of February of the gentlemen named as officers of the assembly of the 10th, in Fanueil Hall, and of a few others who had been actively engaged in getting up that meeting. The members of the Legislature present at this meeting represented that the best feeling with respect to the suffering East Tennesseans prevailed at the State-House, and that the chief difficulty in the way of the grant was the doubt entertained by many members of the constitutional right of the Legislature to make such an appropriation. To aid in the removal of this doubt a memorial affirming the constitutional power, drawn up by Hon. C. G. Loring, and subscribed by Judge Curtis and other eminent jurists, was signed by the persons present at the meeting and ordered to be presented to the two houses. A Committee was also appointed, consisting of Mr. Edward Everett, Hon. R. C. Winthrop, J. Wiley Edmands, Esq., Hon. Judge Russell, and Patrick Donahoe, Esq., to consider and report a plan of proceedings in order to a general subscription. In the mean time it was deemed expedient to suspend the daily announcement of donations which had hitherto been made in the columns of the "Boston Daily Advertiser." No further announcements were accordingly made for some days.

It was soon apparent that this withdrawal of the subject from the public eye would operate unfavorably upon the progress of the fund, and at a meeting of the

Sub-Committee on the 20th, it was voted to recommence the daily announcements, which from this time forward were continued without intermission. But the question of legislative aid being still undecided, it was deemed expedient to postpone for the present a formal appeal to the public.

An inspection of the record of donations for the second week will show with what strength the tide of sympathy and munificence was rising. It would be obviously improper to continue to single out individual cases from the roll of beneficence, but I cannot forbear to allude to the donation of two hundred and fifty dollars from the late venerable Mrs. Pratt, then in the ninety-seventh year of her age, and the liberal contribution of Dr. James Jackson, who gave to the fund, at this early stage, the sanction of his revered name. Mr. William Gray's munificent donation of five hundred dollars was accompanied with a promise of another of the same amount if the legislative grant should fail.

On the 25th, a letter was received from Mr. Speaker Bullock, enclosing the generous donation of one hundred dollars, and announcing the failure of the proposed legislative appropriation in the following terms : —

" COMMONWEALTH OF MASSACHUSETTS,
HOUSE OF REPRESENTATIVES,
Boston, 25th Feb. 1864.

" *My Dear Sir :* — You have already been apprised of the action of the House of Representatives upon the Resolves relating to East Tennessee. I desire that you and all our fellow-citizens should justly appreciate the motives which have controlled the vote of members in refusing the appropriation of $100,000. It is not to be supposed that they are insensible to the sufferings of the people of Tennessee, nor that they have forgotten the pathetic appeal of Colonel Taylor, so fully sustained by the simple and unadorned statement of General Burnside. But, speaking as an impartial witness of the discussion, I may properly say that the members of the House have undoubtedly acted under the influence of grave doubts as to the constitutional propriety of making the appropriation from the State Treasury.

"I take it for granted that this action of the House will render instantly imperative the private contributions of our people. I accordingly inclose to you my own."

*　　　　*　　　　*　　　　*

The failure of the legislative appropriation gave a new impulse to the individual subscriptions. On Saturday, the 27th of February, they exceeded $2,100, and on Monday, the 29th, donations to the amount of more than $4,000 were announced. Among them was the munificent sum of $1,000 contributed by a unanimous vote of the Boston Stock and Exchange Board.

The contributions thus far had been received principally, though not exclusively, from Boston and the immediate vicinity. At a meeting of the Sub-Committee on the 29th of February, it was ordered that the Chairman be requested to prepare the draft of an address to the citizens at large, to be submitted to the General Committee. Accordingly, at a meeting of the General Committee on the 2d of March, a draft of an address was reported by the Chairman, which, with amendments was accepted, as follows. It was thought to indicate the only organization for the collection of subscriptions which was necessary, under the favorable predisposition of the public.

TO THE PEOPLE OF MASSACHUSETTS.

" THE undersigned were appointed a Committee of the citizens of Boston, assembled in Faneuil Hall on the 10th of February, to present the subject of the destitution of our loyal brethren in East Tennessee to the consideration of the Legislature. In the discharge of this duty, the Resolutions adopted by that meeting, with enthusiasm and unanimity, were respectfully transmitted by the undersigned to the House of Representatives. But the wide-spread interest which has been manifested in the subject, by the community at large, and the evident demand for some more organized and concerted action than' has yet taken place, have led the Committee to think they shall render an acceptable service by' addressing themselves directly to the people.

" In doing this, however, they deem it wholly unnecessary to do more than ask the attention of their fellow-citizens, throughout the Commonwealth, to the statements and appeals which have been made with such resistless power by Colonel N. G. Taylor of East Tennessee. Those who have had the privilege of knowing and hearing him, will need no voucher for his character; to others it may not be superfluous to say, that he is fortified with credentials from Governor Johnson of Tennessee and from the President of the United States. Any attempt to add force to his accounts of the distressed condition of his fellow-citizens would be unavailing. The Committee desire only in this Address to suggest to their fellow-citizens convenient methods of giving effect to that warm interest, which they rejoice to believe has been so universally excited in behalf of these noble sufferers.

" They would respectfully propose, therefore, that the municipal authorities of the several cities and towns of the Commonwealth should regard themselves as committees to receive donations from their fellow-citizens; that the churches throughout the State, where no particular reasons exist to the contrary, should take up special collections for this purpose; and that corporate bodies, whose charters allow it to be done and whose means admit, should also contribute to the relief of our destitute brethren.

" Whatever sums may be thus raised may be remitted to the Chair-

man of this Committee, and will, with the large amount already
received, be applied under the direction of the Committee, in the
most prompt and efficient manner.   Contributions will also be most
willingly received by the Chairman of this Committee from liberal
minded individuals, who may wish to take part in this most meritorious and patriotic work, in places where no local committee is organized, or who may for any reason prefer to address themselves to him.

"The Committee trust that it will not be thought obtrusive, in a
case of this kind, if they look beyond the limits of Massachusetts, and
respectfully invite the coöperation of the liberal and patriotic men
and women of the other New England States, either as individuals
or through local committees.   Their contributions, in either case, will
be most willingly received and promptly acknowledged by this Committee.

"The undersigned are happy to state, that, on the application of
the Executive Committee of the Pennsylvania Association for the
relief of East Tennessee, the Secretary of War has promised that the
supplies, which may be forwarded to Nashville, shall be transported
to East Tennessee by the Government trains, and that General Grant
shall be instructed to furnish all possible facilities for their safe con-
veyance.   Articles of food can be most readily obtained in the Western markets; clothing and shoes can probably be procured to greater
advantage in this vicinity.   Donations of these last-named articles
will be most gratefully received, and will be forwarded to their destination by Mr. Samuel Hall, Jr., 8 Central Wharf, Boston.   In the
expenditure of the fund committed to them, the undersigned pledge
their best exertions, that it shall be applied with the utmost possible
economy, promptness, and efficiency.

"In pleading the claims of a class of our fellow-citizens who have
suffered so long and so cruelly, whose patriotism has been so nobly
manifested under the greatest hardships and discouragements, and
whose destitution is now so extreme, the Committee deem it scarcely
becoming to allude to motives of expediency.   But when expediency
runs in the same channel as patriotism, humanity, and conscience, it
may honestly be appealed to.   It may not, therefore, be improper to
state, that in all the field of military operations, there is not a spot of
greater interest and importance than East Tennessee.   As the con-

trol of the Mississippi divides the States in rebellion East and West, so the restoration of East Tennessee to its loyal inhabitants severs one of the two remaining lines of communication between the North and the South of the States confederated in this gigantic treason. There is accordingly no object of greater importance than to maintain this district, which will in all probability be one of the great battle-grounds of the approaching campaign. It hardly need be stated that this circumstance will of necessity complete the exhaustion of the territory, and reduce, if possible, to a still lower depth, the destitution of the entire non-combatant population.

"The Committee will only remark in conclusion, that the case now presented to the public sympathy seems to them to stand alone, in the strength of its appeal to our patriotic liberality. A loyal people, equal in numbers to the entire free population of South Carolina, nobly adhering to the Union by a majority of five to one, when South Carolina took the lead in a treasonable war against it; selected for this reason as an object of vindictive hostility; the vast majority of her citizens denounced by a military Cabal at Richmond as traitors, because they refused to commit treason; her prominent citizens too old for military duty hurried off to perish in the prisons of the Gulf States; her young men forced into the rebel army; Union men, active in opposition to the tyrants who pretend to wage war for self-government and State rights while trampling on both, cruelly scourged and in some instances shot and hung in the sight of their families, their property given up to waste and plunder, their old men, women, and children reduced to want, — these are some of the titles of the loyal people of East Tennessee to our sympathy. And when we add that a great majority of the young men, who during two and a half years that their territory was occupied by the Confederate forces have been able to escape conscription into the rebel army, are now battling for the Union, the Committee feel that they present a case hardly to be paralleled in the annals of patriotism. They are confident that in a community like this, the aged parents, the wives, the sisters of brethren who, under circumstances like these, are sealing their fidelity to the Union with their blood, will not be allowed to perish from want.

"EDWARD EVERETT, JOHN A. ANDREW, FREDERIC W. LINCOLN, Jr., J. E. FIELD, A. H. BULLOCK, ROBERT C. WINTHROP, CHARLES

G. Loring, William Claflin, Patrick Donahoe, W. B. Rogers, Charles B. Goodrich, James Lawrence, Richard Frothingham, John M. Forbes, Thomas Russell, A. A. Lawrence,
J. Wiley Edmands, J. Z. Goodrich, F. L. Lee, Samuel Frothingham.

" *Boston*, March 2, 1864.

" P. S. The Press throughout the Commonwealth is respectfully
requested to give insertion to the foregoing Address."

When the Sub-Committee held their meeting on the
last day of February, the fund exceeded $19,000,
which had been contributed spontaneously and without solicitation, in the seventeen days which had
elapsed from the announcement of "the Teacher's"
modest donation. Steps had been taken, at the out-
set, to ascertain the most direct channel for the con-
veyance of supplies to East Tennessee. In order to
make a portion of the fund as promptly available as
possible, the Sub-Committee, having been clothed with
full powers as an Executive Committee, determined on
the 2d of March to remit $10,000 to Lloyd P. Smith,
Esq., of Philadelphia, who, in conjunction with Frederic Collins, Esq. was about to repair to Knoxville in
person, on behalf of the Pennsylvania Association for
the Relief of East Tennessee. These gentlemen readily
took charge of this sum, and it was joined with the
funds of the Pennsylvania Association, in the purchase
of large supplies of food at Cincinnati. These supplies
were as promptly conveyed to Knoxville, as the means
of transportation at Nashville allowed, almost the entire force of the railroad being required by General
Sherman's army, then on the advance into Georgia.

A very interesting report of the visit of Messrs. Smith and Collins to Knoxville has been published by those gentlemen, and they are entitled to the cordial thanks of the contributors in this part of the country, for their fidelity and good judgment, in the application of the funds remitted from Boston.

From this time forward the fund advanced with perhaps unexampled rapidity. The sum announced on the 3d of March amounted to $6,349, which was the largest sum in any one day. The sum of $4,829 was reported on the 4th; of $3,456 on the 5th; of $5,024 on the 7th; and of $3,120 on the 8th, which included the donation of $1,000 from the officers and men of the 44th Regiment of Massachusetts Volunteers. This handsome donation was accompanied with the following letter : —

"Boston, *March* 5, 1864.

"*Hon. Edward Everett :* Dear Sir, — Through the liberality of their fellow-citizens, the Regiment which I have the honor to command, received a Regimental Fund of $5,000. A portion of this money has been applied to the use of the Regiment, — a portion I retain for further need of the Regiment. Upon consultation with William Gray, Esq., Treasurer of the fund, and with my field-officers, and feeling sure that it will meet the approval of the original donors, I have decided to devote $1,000 to the relief of the suffering loyalists of East Tennessee, which please accept in behalf of the men and officers of the 44th Regiment M. V. M.

"I am, Sir, your obedient servant,

"Francis L. Lee, Col. 44th Regt. M. V. M."

The contributions announced on the 9th of March amounted to $6,220, in which was included the sum of

$4,773 collected in Franklin Street and its vicinity by the active exertions of George H. Braman, Esq. In a supplement to the "Boston Daily Advertiser" of the 9th of March, a complete list was given of all the donations up to the 8th, amounting in the aggregate to $52,120 received in less than a month from the date of the meeting in Faneuil Hall.

On the 5th of March, Messrs. J. Ingersoll Bowditch, Hon. A. A. Lawrence, and Samuel Hall, Jr., Esq., were added to the Executive Committee. Mr. Hall kindly took charge of the contributions of ready-made clothing, &c. and forwarded them from time to time to their destination. His reports will be given in the sequel and will show how much the cause is indebted to him for his laborious and gratuitous services.

It having been intimated by Mrs. George Ticknor, President of the Ladies' Sewing Circle, that the ladies of that association would cheerfully make up into articles of wearing apparel such materials as the Committee would furnish for that purpose, it was voted on the 10th of March to place the sum of $2,000 at her disposal, to be expended in the purchase of materials. In this way, the sum appropriated was, by the generous coöperation of the Ladies' Sewing Circle, rendered nearly twice as efficient as it would otherwise have been. The articles of clothing made up were forwarded from time to time by Mr. Hall. The extent of the labor bestowed by the Ladies' Sewing Circle may be seen in the following report of its results : —

" *Dear Mr. Everett:* — It is due to you, to the gentlemen who consented to intrust us with $2,000, and to us who received the trust, that some report should be made of the mode in which we have used the money given for the benefit of sufferers in Tennessee. We have used it as discreetly and carefully as we could ; — we sent last Monday our *ninth* package to Mr. Hall, the agent you designated, and that exhausted the last dollar of our fund.

"The schedule of the packages is as follows : —

Whole number of articles sent	2,921
Whole number procured by $2,000	2,579
Donations, and socks knit from the yarn sent by Mr. Edmands	342
	2,921
Of this number there were : —	
For women and children	1,875
For men and boys	1,046

"It has been a very interesting occupation, and we wish we could do more for those who suffer so terribly and so faithfully.

"Hoping you will think that we have fulfilled our stewardship suitably, we are very truly yours,

"ANNA TICKNOR,

"*Park Street*, June 8, 1864."   "ISA E. LORING."

I subjoin a letter from Rev. Dr. Humes, Chairman of the Knoxville East Tennessee Relief Association, containing a copy of a vote of thanks adopted at a regular meeting of the Executive Committee, on the receipt of the foregoing report.

"KNOXVILLE, Tenn., *June* 22, 1864.

"*Dear Sir:* — At the regular meeting of the Executive Committee of the East Tennessee Relief Association, held to-day, it was unanimously

"'*Resolved*, That the Chairman be instructed to tender the thanks of this Society to Mrs. Ticknor and Miss Loring, and to the Ladies of the Sewing Circle of Boston, whom they represent, for their kind sympathy and benevolent labors, on behalf of the destitute and suffering people of East Tennessee; and that this insufficient tribute to their active patriotism and friendship be placed upon the records of the Committee, in token, not only of gratitude, but also of our desire

that the memory of their names and good deeds be cherished and per-
petuated in our mountain homes, long after the garments, with which
they have clothed their needy countrymen, shall have perished.'

" I need scarcely say that it gives me peculiar pleasure to comply
with the directions of the Committee, and to communicate, as I beg
leave to do through you, to Mrs. Ticknor and Miss Loring, a copy of
the above resolution of thanks.

" With the assurance of my strong and sincere appreciation of their
practical good will, I am,

" Yours truly and respectfully,

" THOMAS W. HUMES,

" Chairman Ex. Com. E. T. R. A."

In thus placing on record the active coöperation of
the Ladies' Sewing Circle, I cannot forbear adverting
to the large share borne generally by the patriotic
women of the community in this meritorious work.
An inspection of the list of donations will show them
to have been among the earliest and most liberal contributors; and I am well persuaded that their active
sympathy, felt in every form of domestic influence,
has been one of the most efficient causes of the success
of the efforts for the relief of our suffering brethren in
East Tennessee. There were incidents and circumstances of the war, as it bore upon the women of that
devoted region, well calculated to touch the hearts of
their sisters in the loyal States. Husbands, brothers,
and sons were often torn from their homes, thrown
into prison, forced into the army, in some cases shot
or hung in sight of their families. The following
touching occurrence of a different character was
vouched for by Colonel Taylor, as within his own
knowledge.

"INCIDENT OF THE WAR. — After the battle at Bean 'Station, East Tennessee, the rebels were guilty of all manner of indignity toward the slain. They stripped their bodies, and shot all persons who came near the battle-field to show any attention to the dead. The body of a little drummer-boy was left naked and exposed. Near by, in an humble house, there were two young girls, the eldest but sixteen, who resolved to give the body a decent burial. They took the night for their task. With hammer and nails in hand, and boards on their shoulders, they sought the place where the body of the dead drummer-boy lay. From their own scanty wardrobe, they clothed the body for the grave. With their own hands they made a rude coffin, into which they reverently put the dead boy. They dug the grave, and lowered the body into it and covered it over. The noise of the hammer brought some of the rebels to the spot. The sight was too much for them. The stillness of the night — the story so eloquently told by the heroic labors of the little girls. Not a word was spoken ; no one interfered, and when the sacred rites of burial were performed, all separated ; and the little drummer-boy sleeps undisturbed in his grave on the battle-field."

The most judicious and efficient manner of disposing of the fund was of course an object of early consideration with the Committee. They were aware that strong objections to the employment of salaried agents, for the disbursement of a fund of this kind, existed in the community, although in some cases the duty cannot be so satisfactorily performed through any other agency. To entertain individual applications for relief coming from so great a distance was out of the question. Fortunately there already existed at Knoxville, the capital of East Tennessee, an Association organized for the purpose of relieving the distress of that devoted region. The gentlemen composing the Executive Committee of that Association[1] were certified to us as persons of the highest respectability, and the Committee conceived that they should best discharge their duty to the generous contributors to the fund, by paying it over in large instalments and as fast as it could be advantageously invested, to the accredited agents of the Knoxville Relief Association, who were duly authorized to receive it. These agents, at that time, were Colonel N. G. Taylor, to the effect of whose fervid appeals the formation of the fund was mainly due, and Mr. G. M. Hazen of Knoxville. A letter having been received from Colonel Taylor, then in New York, requesting that the funds on hand might be remitted to him and Mr. Hazen, it was on the 17th of March voted by the Executive Committee, that Mr. J. Wiley Edmands, one of their number who was about to visit New York, be requested to examine the credentials of Messrs. Taylor and Hazen. If in his judgment they were found sufficient, the Chairman was authorized to accept their draft for a sum not exceeding $40,000. Mr. Edmands found the gentlemen named to be clothed with full authority to receive and invest whatever funds might be contributed for relief of the loyal people of East Tennessee. Accordingly on the 21st of March their draft at sight for $40,000 was paid.

Mr. Hazen repaired immediately to Cincinnati, the nearest market to East Tennessee, at which provisions

---

[1] This Committee consisted of Rev. Dr. Humes, (a clergyman of the Episcopal Church, possessing the entire confidence of the community,) Messrs. William Heiskell, W. G. Brownlow, John Baxter, O. P. Temple, and John M. Fleming.

could be obtained, and invested the fund placed in his hands by the Committee and a small sum which had been collected by Colonel Taylor, in those articles which were most needed for the relief of the existing distress. On the arrival of this large amount of flour and other bread-stuffs, bacon, and other articles of food at Nashville, considerable delay arose from the limited means of transportation, the railroad to Chattanooga being the only route. The War Department, as has been observed, had, at the instance of the Pennsylvania Committee, engaged to coöperate in the relief of East Tennessee, and to allow supplies to go forward by the Government trains. The exigencies of the military service required at first the employment of the entire force of the railroad, but before long the agent of the Knoxville Relief Committee was allowed to dispose of one merchandise car daily, or to that average amount. In this way the supplies were conveyed to their destination as rapidly as they could be advantageously received and distributed.

This distribution was effected in the most satisfactory manner. Under the superintendence of the Executive Committee at Knoxville, local committees were organized in the different counties in East Tennessee within the federal lines. It was, of course, impossible to send supplies into those counties in the Northeastern part of the State, which were in the possession of the enemy, and not entirely safe to do so, in the middle region, lying open to the ravages of armed bands of ruffians under the name of guerrillas. But fugitives from these districts constantly arriving at Knoxville were relieved at that place. A small portion of the supplies were sold at Knoxville and elsewhere to persons who had money, but owing to the destitution of the markets, were unable to exchange it for food. The Committee here did not recommend this measure, but there seems to be no valid objection to it, as without it persons having the means to purchase would in some 'localities have been obliged to accept as a gift what they would rather pay for. The proceeds of these sales were of course added by the Knoxville Committee to their funds.

On·the 20th of April, the further sum of $20,000 was, on the draft of Colonel Taylor, remitted to Gilmore, Dunlap & Co., bankers of the Knoxville Relief Association at Cincinnati. The funds intrusted to us having been all contributed under the influence of the eloquent appeals of Colonel Taylor, deputed by the Knoxville Committee to procure relief for his fellow-citizens of East Tennessee, were evidently applicable exclusively to that object, nor could they justly be extended to sufferers in any other quarter, though equally destitute and meritorious. Accordingly when representations were made to us by letter of the great distress among the loyal refugees at Murfreesborough, and still more at Nashville and even at Cincinnati, though principally at Nashville, knowing that these refugees had fled not only from East Tennessee, but from Western North Carolina and the Northern counties of the Gulf States, profoundly sympathizing as we did with the sufferers at the places just named, and fully aware of the heavy burden which had devolved upon our fellow-citizens at Nashville, we yet felt it beyond our power to adopt any general measure of relief. We called the attention, however, of the Knoxville Committee to the subject, and suggested the expediency of authorizing a reasonable distribution of supplies at Murfreesborough for fugitives from East Tennessee, and such relief as might be deemed practicable to the much larger number of the same class at Nashville and Cincinnati. This recommendation was promptly and liberally complied with by the Knoxville Committee.

About the middle of April a communication was addressed to the Secretary of War, setting forth that the transportation of supplies, notwithstanding the kind promise of the Department, was seriously delayed at Nashville, and requesting that if this arose from any undue strictness in construing the orders which gave precedence to the Government work, the officer in charge might be directed to interpret them more liberally. To this letter the following reply was received from the Department: —

"WAR DEPARTMENT,
"WASHINGTON CITY, May 4, 1864.

"*Sir :* — I have the honor, by direction of the Secretary of War, to acknowledge the receipt of your communication of the 24th ultimo, relating to the difficulty experienced in obtaining transportation for the supplies furnished by citizens of Massachusetts, for the benefit of suffering Unionists in East Tennessee.

"In reply, I am instructed to say that these difficulties arise solely from the fact, that every available means of transportation has been, and is still, needed by General Sherman, to transport supplies of food for his army, preparatory to the opening of the Spring Campaign. In the mean time, Government rations have, whenever practicable, been issued in cases of special need, (230,000 rations have already been issued in such cases in the department of the Tennessee,) and you may rest assured that the facilities desired by you, will be furnished, whenever the interest and the necessities of the public service will permit.

" I have the honor to be, Sir, very respectfully,

" Your obedient servant,

[Signed] ED. R. S. CANBY, Brigadier-General.

" HON. EDWARD EVERETT, Boston, Mass."

Meantime the fund continued to increase. The sympathy in which it had its origin pervaded all classes of the community. Donations continued to be made, from those of a thousand dollars and more from the Stock and Exchange Board, the Corn Exchange, and the ladies and gentlemen who took part in the musical entertainments at Chickering's Hall, down to the literal mite of the poor widow. Other dramatic exhibitions, concerts, and exhibitions of tableaux contributed liberal sums. Children's fairs were held in town and country, the proceeds of two of which amounted to $1,000 each, and several churches took up large collections, notwithstanding the liberal donations already made by individual members. The principal amount received was from Massachusetts, although some handsome remittances were made from Providence, R. I., from New Hampshire, from Maine, Vermont, and New York. Among these it will not be thought improper for me to mention the donations of $500 each from Mrs. Deborah Powers of Lansingburg, N. Y., Miss Arabella Rice of Portsmouth, N. H., and Hon. J. Goodwin of Portsmouth, from the estate of the late Mrs. Charlotte

Rice of that place, and in presumed accordance with what would have been her wishes.

In this way the fund which, when the aggregate list was published on the 9th of March, amounted to above $52,000, had by the end of that month swelled to above $77,000. The end of April brought it up to $91,500. One hundred thousand dollars, the amount of the appropriation proposed in the Legislature, had been assigned by public opinion as the sum which we should endeavor to raise by private subscription, and on the 4th of June that amount was reached. The foundation was laid in the Teacher's donation of three dollars on the 11th of February, the head-stone was carried up by $1,000 received from a Children's Fair at the house of Dr. T. I. Talbot on the 4th of June. On the following morning the fact was announced in the "Daily Advertiser," with the following remarks:—

"To the numerous individuals and societies whose unsolicited donations have resulted in this large contribution for the relief of our loyal and destitute brethren in East Tennessee, on their behalf I return my most grateful acknowledgments.

"In addition to the sum of one hundred thousand dollars, thus contributed in money, articles of clothing valued in the aggregate at some thousands have been received and forwarded. Nor must the assiduous labor of the Ladies' Boston Sewing Circle, in making up two thousand dollars worth of materials of clothing, and of other smaller sewing circles, in town and country, be forgotten.

"Liberal as is the amount, which has thus far been raised, here and elsewhere, much destitution and suffering will still remain unrelieved. I shall be most happy, on behalf of the Committee, whose organ I have the honor to be, still to receive whatever may be contributed for this object, announcing the donations, however, less frequently than has hitherto been done.

"It is but an act of justice to the Editors of the "Daily Advertiser" to return them the cordial thanks of the Committee for the gratuitous daily insertion of my announcements, at one time of great length, for which the usage of the Press would have warranted the ordinary advertising charge. The success of the subscription has, in no small degree, been promoted by this liberality on their part.

"EDWARD EVERETT."

I am happy to state that more than two thousand dollars have since been added to the fund.

The following reports from Mr. Hall will afford some idea of the quantity of ready-made clothing which has been forwarded by that gentleman. The pecuniary value of the articles has been stated but in few instances, but is supposed to amount to several thousand dollars. Sincere thanks are due to Mr. Hall for his laborious and gratuitous services in forwarding them.

"*Dear Sir :* — The following packages, containing clothing, &c., have been received to this date, contributed for the sufferers in East Tennessee, viz : —

1 box from Mrs. Ticknor, Park Street.
1 bundle from M. G. Chapman.
1 do. from Mrs. H. F. Damon.
1 do. from Mrs. Sherman.
1 box, value $250, from Mrs. J. A. Little, President of the Ladies' Union of Arlington Street Church.
1 bundle from Mrs. Balch.
4 do. from Mrs. E. Atkins.
1 do. from Mrs. Emory Washburn, Cambridge.
2 do. from the Misses Ward.
1 do. from Dr. Winsor, Cambridge.
1 do. from Mrs. Emerson.
1 do. from Miss Wells, Cambridge.
1 do. from Mrs. Pickering.

1 bundle from John Gardner.
1 do. from Prof. F. J. Child, Cambridge.
2 boxes from Melendy & Stewart.
3 barrels and 1 bundle from ladies of West Medford, through Mrs. Eliza H. Caret.
2 bundles from George F. Guild.
1 do. from Mr. Clark.
1 do. from Mrs. Frances Parkman.
2 boxes from Mr. R. Pollard.
1 do. from J. C. Hoadly, New Bedford.
2 bundles from Mrs. Dr. Charles E. Ware.
12 do. from persons unknown.

"Respectfully yours,

"SAMUEL HALL, JR.

"BOSTON, *March* 24, 1864."

"*Dear Sir :* — The following contributions of clothing, &c. for the sufferers in East Tennessee have been received since my last acknowledgment (March 24), and have been sent forward, viz : —

3 boxes and 2 bundles from Boston Sewing Circle, by Mrs. Ticknor.
1 bundle from Mrs. McNeil, Roxbury.
1 do. Miss C. A. Brewer.
1 do. Mrs. Thwing, Quincy.
1 do. S. Chapin, Gloucester.
1 do. B. F. Adams.
1 do. Mr. Bullard.
2 do. L. A. Huntington.
1 do. William P. Thurston, Jamaica Plain, and 21 Dover street.
2 cases brogans from Col. Gordon McKay.
1 bundle from Edward Page.
1 box and 1 bundle from the Industrial Society of St. Paul's Church.
1 do. from Miss I. E. Loring.
8 bundles from Mr. Manning.
8 barrels and 2 boxes from John J. May.

1 bundle from Mrs. Sarah Johnson, value $33.
2 boxes from Waltham Soldiers' Aid Society, by Miss M. J. Miles, value $375.
1 basket and 1 bundle from Miss Margaret C. Thompson.
1 bundle from Mrs. C. E. Norton, Cambridge.
2 boxes from J. H. Nichols, Salem.
2 bundles from Mrs. Augustus Flagg.
1 do. from "A New Bedford Lady."
2 boxes and 1 bundle from "Corner of Summer and Otis streets."
2 bundles from Bishop Eastburn.
2 do. from Rev. Mr. Foote.
1 box from North Bridgewater.
2 boxes and a bundle from Mr. Joseph Willard.

"Respectfully yours,

"SAMUEL HALL, JR.

"*April* 18, 1864."

"BOSTON, *May* 18, 1864.

"*Dear Sir :* — Since my last acknowledgment (April 18th), the following contributions of clothing, &c., have been received, all of which have been forwarded to the sufferers of East Tennessee, viz : —

3 cases from Boston Sewing Circle, by Mrs. Ticknor.
2 bundles from Mrs. Fletcher.
1 bundle unknown.
1 box from New Bedford.
1 bundle from Mrs. McKean.
1 case from ladies of Beverley, by Hannah C. Adams.
2 bundles from Mrs. T. C. Hubbard, Newton.

1 box from Greenfield, or Shelburne Falls.
1 bundle from Mrs. Atkins.
1 barrel, value $53.75, from Ladies' Benevolent Society, Amory Village, Millbury, Mass.
1 bundle, 80 pairs stockings, J. Wiley Edmands.
1 do. from Miss Minot.
1 box from Salem.
1 bundle from R. H. Stearns.

"Respectfully yours,

"SAMUEL HALL, JR."

" Boston, *June* 24, 1864.

" *Dear Sir:* — Since my last report (May 18), the following packages of clothing, &c., have been received, all of which have been forwarded to the East Tennessee Relief Association, viz : —

2 boxes from Boston Sewing Circle, by Mrs. Ticknor.	1 bundle, Moses P. Grant.
1 box, New Church Sewing Circle, Boston.	1 do. Rev. Mr. Barnes, Malden.
	1 do. Mr. Morrill.
1 do. Brookfield, Mass.	1 do. Mrs. Curret, West Medford.
1 do. and 2 baskets, Louisburg Square.	1 do. H. Williams.
	1 do. Mrs. Eastburn.

" Respectfully yours,

" Samuel Hall, Jr."

In this connection it may be proper to mention that Mr. Allen Cameron, agent of the Abbot Worsted Company, Graniteville, contributed one hundred pounds of gray stocking yarn, worth one dollar and fifty cents per pound, to be knit for the destitute in East Tennessee. A portion of this yarn was knit into eighty pairs of stockings by the ladies of Rev. Edward E. Hale's congregation.

After Mr. Hazen had invested at Cincinnati the sum remitted to him and Colonel Taylor as above mentioned, he was relieved of his agency, and Thomas G. Odiorne, Esq. of Cincinnati, was appointed by the Executive Committee at Knoxville, as their permanent purchasing agent. This gentleman's residence at Cincinnati, high character, disinterested zeal in the cause, and experience as the agent of the Sanitary Commission eminently qualified him for the efficient discharge of the trust, which he has executed to the entire satisfaction of the Committee in Boston and the Executive Committee at Knoxville.

It has already been stated, that, instead of employing paid agents of their own, the Committee deemed it expedient, from time to time, to pay over the fund intrusted to them to the accredited agents of the Knoxville Relief Association. By April the 23d, $72,000 had been advanced in this way.[1] This sum, with the liberal appropriation of the Philadelphia Committee, and donations made directly to Colonel Taylor, has kept the agent at Cincinnati amply supplied with funds for the purchase of all the supplies, which could be sent forward by water to Nashville, and has left a balance in his hands to be invested in proportion as transportation can be obtained by the Louisville and Nashville Railroad.

On the 28th of July, the fund intrusted to the Committee having reached an amount larger by about $2,000 than the sum originally contemplated, a meeting was called to consider the expediency of closing the account, and it was decided that of the balance on hand, $28,000 should be remitted to the bankers at Cincinnati, making $100,000 paid over, and leaving the residue chargeable with the cost of transportation of the ready-made clothing, forwarded by Mr. Hall, and some small contingent expenses. Before the remittance could take place, a letter was received from Dr. Humes, stating that the stock of supplies on hand at Knoxville, and in charge of the local agents would, with prudent management, suffice till larger

---

[1] In this sum of $72,000 are included $10,000 paid to the Philadelphia Committee, and $2,000 expended in materials of clothing made up by the Ladies' Sewing Circle.

means of transportation could be obtained; and that
as the number of refugees at Knoxville was increasing,
it was expedient to have in reserve the means of relief
for autumn and winter, when he fears, that the distress
will again become serious. For these reasons, he rec-
ommends that the Committee should retain, for the
present, the balance in their hands. In accordance
with this advice he has been informed that $28,000
will be held by the Committee subject to his draft at
sight, or that of the bankers at Cincinnati acting by
his direction.

It is but an act of justice to the Knoxville Committee to speak in terms of high commendation of the
manner in which they have effected the distribution of
the supplies, — a work beset with no inconsiderable
difficulties arising from the extent of territory to be
relieved, the want of those means of communication
which *exist in most of the Atlantic States, and the
unsettled state of the country. By the aid of local
organizations and agencies, with the vigilant super-
vision of the Central Committee at Knoxville, it is
believed that the work has been judiciously and satisfactorily performed. Some losses have occurred, una-
voidable it is presumed, on a line of communication so
extensive and circuitous, where delay and irregularity
in transportation were necessarily accompanied with
unexpected accumulation at particular points, and
where the channels of ultimate distribution are so
numerous. But the Committee have no reason to
think that these losses were greater than was to be

expected under the circumstances of the case, the nature of the service, and the state of the country.

The Committee perform an agreeable duty in acknowledging their special obligations to the Rev. Dr. Humes, the Chairman of the Executive Committee of the East Tennessee Relief Association. Too much cannot be said in praise of the diligence, fulness, and punctuality of his correspondence. The extracts from it, which have accompanied the daily announcement of donations, have served an important purpose in keeping up the public interest in the cause. It has afforded the contributors to the fund the satisfaction of knowing that their active sympathy has taken the desired effect; and that the supplies so liberally furnished have been faithfully and judiciously distributed.

Dr. Humes' letters have not only furnished the satisfactory information of suffering relieved, want of the most urgent kind supplied, and of life no doubt in this way, in many cases preserved, but they have contained assurances scarcely less gratifying that the moral effect upon the minds of our fellow-citizens in East Tennessee of this manifestation of active sympathy on the part of their Northern brethren has been most auspicious. It has impressed them with feelings toward their fellow-citizens of the North not soon to be effaced. It has shown them that the love of the Union with us is not a profession which satisfies itself with words but a sentiment which warms the heart.

The following, with the omission of some personal allusions, is extracted from the "Knoxville Whig" of the 25th of June last: —

" In a late letter from Mr. Everett to the President of the East Tennessee Relief Association, the fact is announced that Massachusetts has contributed ONE HUNDRED THOUSAND DOLLARS for the relief of the suffering and destitute people of East Tennessee. . . . This is one of the most remarkable and suggestive facts developed by this strange war. Between Tennessee and Massachusetts there has never been any common identity of habit or thought, and no close commercial or personal ties, which sometimes bind together the citizens of neighboring States. Indeed, we have been taught for many years (though we did not all believe) that the people of the North were narrow-minded, selfish, cold, and avaricious. But no sooner do they hear the tale of the destitution of a people fifteen hundred miles away, than, with the instincts of a common humanity, a common religion, and a common patriotism, they outstrip all others in the most generous race of charity."

After alluding to the coöperation of " all the leading men and all the churches, charitable associations, public and private institutions, and of the women, the boys, and the girls," the article proceeds : —

" No one seems to have felt that he had done his duty unless he had contributed something. And all this was done from principle, not from enthusiasm. They regarded it as a sacred duty. They ever have been taught that charity and benevolence are duties which they cannot neglect. The Southern gentleman, rolling in his wealth, will live in the greatest elegance, and expend his money with princely prodigality on himself and his own circle, but he has a dull ear to the claims of charity outside of his circle. He is most liberal to himself, while the Northern man is more liberal to others. Herein is the difference between the two. Hence public enterprises have been fostered and patronized, and the cold and bleak North has prospered and grown great ; while the rich and productive South has stood comparatively still for want of that liberal public enterprise.

" We say, from the bottom of our heart, all honor to glorious old Massachusetts. The people of that State are indeed our neighbors and our brethren. And that which is true of them is likewise true, possibly in a less degree, of all the people of the North. For, even far-off Maine has generously contributed her thousands for the relief of our suffering people. And so of nearly every State. Let us hold them in everlasting remembrance, and prove ourselves worthy of their benefactions."

Respectfully submitted, by order of the Committee, to the contributors to the fund, by

EDWARD EVERETT.

P. S. — Since the foregoing Report was prepared, the further sum of twenty thousand five hundred dollars ($20,500) was, on the 3d of October, remitted to the Bankers of the Knoxville East Tennessee Relief Association, and an order filled for shoes to the amount of seven thousand five hundred dollars ($7,500), to be forwarded to Knoxville, making, with the sums above reported, an aggregate of one hundred thousand dollars ($100,000).

LIST OF CONTRIBUTORS.

LIST OF CONTRIBUTORS

FUND FOR THE RELIEF OF THE LOYAL AND SUFFERING EAST TENNESSEEANS.

Feb. 11,	Teacher of a Public School	$3 00
Feb. 12,	F. H. Peabody	100 00
"	Lt.-Col. Peabody	50 00
"	Boston Boy	5 00
Feb. 13,	Mrs. Sylvester Baker, jr., Yarmouth Port	5 00
Feb. 15,	James Gordon Clarke	50 00
"	Mrs. S. Hooper	100 00
"	A lady aged 83	5 00
Feb. 16,	Mrs. John Mackay	100 00
"	Anonymous	20 00
"	Anonymous	5 00
"	Charles P. Curtis	50 00
Feb. 17,	A friend	50 00
"	A Bank Clerk	3 00
"	For the destitute Tennesseans	20 00
"	Anonymous	5 00
"	Augustus Lowell	100 00
"	E. A. Raymond	30 00
"	Dorchester 1791, dated at Newton	200 00
"	W. H. Gardiner	200 00
Feb. 18,	Elisha T. Loring	100 00
"	General James Dana, Charlestown	50 00
Feb. 19,	An old lady	50 00
"	Anonymous	4 00
"	Mrs. E. Wigglesworth	100 00
"	Octavius Pickering	30 00
Feb. 20,	A poor girl	1 00
"	Anonymous	2 00
Feb. 21,	Anonymous — a lady	100 00
Feb. 22,	Dr. James Jackson	50 00
	Carried up	$1588 00

Feb. 22,	Brought up	$1588 00
"	Children's Fair in Mt. Vernon Street	100 00
"	John Gardner	50 00
"	William Everett	20 00
"	W. F. Weld	100 00
"	Dr. John Homans	100 00
"	Mrs. William Pratt	250 00
"	Mrs. G. H. Shaw	250 00
"	Anonymous, Jamaica Plain	50 00
"	Anonymous	5 00
Feb. 23,	Sprague, Soule & Co.	500 00
"	Anonymous	50 00
"	Anonymous	50 00
"	Anonymous	5 00
"	Anonymous, Salem	100 00
"	Edmund Munroe	50 00
"	Ladies of Needham Plain	52 00
"	Lydia S. Gale	100 00
"	J. C. Hoadley, New Bedford	48 00
"	Mrs. Henry Grew	100 00
"	C. S. F., Keene, N. H.	20 00
"	Nathaniel Francis	200 00
"	A Scotch woman	10 00
Feb. 24,	Ignatius Sargent, Machias, Me., the contribution of loyal citizens	100 00
"	Abbott Lawrence	200 00
"	James Parker	100 00
"	Henry W. Pickering	50 00
"	Miss Charlotte Harris	100 00
	Carried over	$4348 00

Feb. 24,	Brought over......	$4348 00
"	Miss Isa E. Loring..	200 00
"	Miss F. L. Gray.....	25 00
"	Miss A. G. Gray....	20 00
"	William Gray.......	500 00
"	George Howe.......	200 00
"	Annie..............	3 00
"	A child.............	1 00
"	W. Yarmouth.......	1 00
Feb. 25,	Mrs. G. Lee........	100 00
"	A lady in Chestnut Street............	25 00
"	James Sturgis.......	50 00
"	P. C. Brooks........	200 00
"	Thomas J. Lee......	50 00
"	Master Reginald Gray	5 00
"	" Sam. S. Gray.	5 00
"	Wm. T. Andrews...	100 00
"	Dr. Charles Mifflin ..	50 00
"	Miss Louisa M. Goddard..............	50 00
"	C. G., a poor man's offering	5 00
"	Hon. A. H. Bullock .	100 00
"	William S. Rogers ..	50 00
"	Mrs. Abby M. Wales	50 00
"	Miss Wales.........	300 00
"	Anonymous.........	50 00
"	Anonymous.........	50 00
"	Anonymous.........	20 00
"	Friend X...........	100 00
Feb. 26,	Mrs. Sally Batchelder	5 00
"	W. W. Clapp, jr.....	25 00
"	Hon. George B. Upton	200 00
"	A Salem lady.......	100 00
"	George M. Wales....	100 00
"	Rev. Dr. Burroughs.	50 00
"	Mrs. Dr. Hayward, Pemberton Square.	100 00
"	Hon. Dwight Foster.	50 00
"	Master Willie R. Richards	10 00
"	Charles Deane......	100 00
"	Sam. Boyd, Marlboro'	100 00
"	Joseph Whitney & Co.	100 00
"	Jonathan Ellis & Co.	100 00
"	Mrs. B. D. Greene ..	200 00
"	George Livermore, Cambridge........	100 00
"	Sterne Morse	100 00
"	Rev. Dr. N. L. Frothingham...........	50 00
"	Turner Sargent.....	100 00
"	Richard Leeds	50 00
"	Johnson & Thompson	100 00
"	A friend from Brookline	50 00
"	J. C. Tyler & Co....	100 00
"	C. D. Head & T. H. Perkins...........	100 00
	Carried up......,..	$8648 00

Feb. 26,	Brought up........	$8648 00
"	O. S. O.............	20 00
"	A Bostonian	2 00
Feb. 27,	Dr. John Ware......	50 00
"	John Wooldredge...	100 00
"	Boston Stock and Exchange Board, by unanimous vote ...	1000 00
"	A Friend...........	10 00
"	Charles E. Guild....	25 00
"	Hon. Jacob Sleeper..	100 00
"	Messrs. H. & L. Chase	50 00
"	Matthew Howland, New Bedford	50 00
"	Samuel Johnson.....	100 00
"	Mrs. Thomas G. Cary	100 00
"	A lady	20 00
"	B. C. Ward........	100 00
"	John J. Low, West Roxbury	25 00
"	Rev. Wm. Mountfort	50 00
"	A poor ex-Teacher..	2 00
"	James M. Beebe.....	200 00
"	Joseph B. Glover....	100 00
"	Robert Waterston...	100 00
"	J. Huntington Wolcott	200 00
"	Mrs. Wolcott.......	100 00
"	J. Randolph Coolidge	50 00
"	Hon. Stephen Fairbanks.............	100 00
"	Hon. C. G. Loring..	100 00
"	The Misses Lowell, Roxbury	200 00
"	Mrs. Mary B. Parkman..............	25 00
"	Geo................	5 00
"	Miss Eliza S. Quincy	50 00
"	C. H. Gay..........	25 00
"	Martin L. Bradford..	50 00
"	R. C. Mackay.......	150 00
"	W. Mackay.........	50 00
"	Newton	20 00
"	W. from Newton....	5 00
"	James Hunnewell, Charlestown	100 00
"	Rebecca P. Allyn, Cambridge	20 00
"	Carruth & Sweetser .	100 00
"	Col. Charles R. Codman	50 00
"	G. L.	35 00
"	Jacob Stone, Newburyport	20 00
"	Col. Theodore Lyman	100 00
"	A. S. Stimpson	25 00
"	Master Stimpson, a birthday offering ..	2 00
"	K Street............	6 00
"	Anonymous.........	15 00
	Carried over....$12,455 00

Feb. 27, Brought over..... $12,455 00
" Clara and Lucy Rogers, twin sisters... 30 00
" Martin Brimmer.... 250 00
" Master Edward Gray 8 00
" Mrs. Eliza Babcock.. 20 00
" A lady in Greenfield, Mass............. 10 00
" Mrs. Henry W. Pickering 50 00
" Harry Pickering 10 00
" Thos. Wigglesworth. 100 00
" Miss Mary Wigglesworth 100 00
" Hon. Charles Allen.. 25 00
" Dr. R. W. Hooper... 100 00
" Mrs. E. Hooper 100 00
" Miss E. Hooper 50 00
" Miss M. I. Hooper .. 50 00
" Miss Ellen S. Hooper 50 00
" Marian Hooper...... 50 00
" J. H. Eastburn...... 100 00
" Solomon Piper...... 100 00
" Jacob A. Dresser.... 50 00
" John Collamore..... 50 00
" J. Wiley Edmands... 500 00
" Mrs. E. R. Mudge... 50 00
" From the Sec. Church in Dorchester, of which from Mrs. Walter Baker $100, and from the Misses Oliver $50* 325 00
" Mason G. Parker.... 25 00
" George H. Tilton.... 25 00
" William W. Tucker. 100 00
" Field, Converse & Allen.............. 100 00
" Miss Eliz'th S. Bangs 30 00
" An aged lady....... 30 00
" J. Eliot Cabot....... 50 00
" Dresser, Stevens & Co............... 50 00
" J. E. Thayer & Bro. 300 00
" W. B. Spooner...... 200 00
" G. B. Cary......... 50 00

Carried up..... $15,543 00

* The donation from the Second Church in Dorchester was accompanied with the following note: —

"DORCHESTER, 29th Feb., 1864.

"DEAR SIR, — I have the pleasure of transmitting to you $325, a contribution for the Patriots of East Tennessee from friends in the Second Church, Dorchester. We observe a fourth Sabbath evening of each month as a time for prayer for our country, and last evening thought it fitting to act as well as pray.

"With much respect I am,
"Dear Sir, truly yours,
[Signed] "JAMES A. MEANS, Pastor."

7 *

Feb. 27, Brought up...... $15,543 00
" Sydney Bartlett..... 100 00
" J. Appleton Burnham 100 00
" Chas. Hook Appleton 100 00
" Charles Amory...... 100 00
" Patrick Donahue.... 100 00
" S. P. H............. 25 00
" Rev. C. T. Thayer.. 50 00
" Rice, Kendall & Co.. 100 00
" J. C. Howe & Co....1000 00
" A crumb for the hungry Tennesseeans . 1 00
" Jos. S. Fay........ 100 00
" H. P. Sturgis....... 100 00
" Henry Lee.......... 100 00
" Henry Lee, jr. 50 00
" Mrs. Henry Lee, jr... 50 00
" W. H. Guild........ 50 00
" Three workwomen.. 7 00
" E. Mudge, Sawyer & Co.............. 500 00
" Col. Samuel Swett... 40 00
Feb. 29, Benjamin S. Rotch.. 100 00
" A Cordial Sympathizer 30 00
" Mrs. C. G. Loring... 100 00
" Hon. J. C. Dodge, Cambridge 50 00
" Henry Upham 100 00
" William Parsons 100 00
" Rev. Henry W. Foote 30 00
" Albert D. Bosson, Chelsea (aged 10).. 1 00
" A Bostonian........ 25 00
" Josiah Quincy, jr.... 100 00
" Prof. F. J. Child, Cambridge.......... 25 00
" W. S. Bullard....... 250 00
" Hon. Artemas Hale, Bridgewater 20 00
" Two ladies, do...... 15 00
" Chas. Brewer & Co... 100 00
" Alexander Moseley.. 100 00
" A Boarder, 44 Summer Street........ 5 00
March 1, Daniel Hammond ... 50 00
" Alfred Winsor & Son 100 00
" A friend............ 30 00
" G. W. Bond........ 100 00
" Dr. Charles E. Ware. 50 00
" James O. Safford.... 100 00
" C. H............... 5 00
" G. A. R............. 10 00
" Dr. Jacob Bigelow... 150 00
" William A. Grover... 100 00
" William S. Whitwell. 50 00
" Two widows........ 10 00
" William Durant..... 100 00
" Mrs. J. Augustus Peabody 50 00

Carried over.... $20,272 00

March 1,	Brought over.....	$20,272 00
"	Mrs. C. Wm. Loring.	50 00
"	Thomas G. Appleton	100 00
"	Mrs. N. Fairbanks ..	5 00
"	Miss Ellen M. Ward.	100 00
"	Miss Julia E. Ward,.	100 00
"	Harrison P. Page, Watertown	100 00
"	Dr. Chas. Beck, Cambridge............	100 00
"	Mrs. Anna S. Möring	25 00
"	T. W. Wellington, Worcester........	50 00
"	From a lady, Salem .	50 00
"	From a merchant, Salem	50 00
"	Mrs. M. Lowell Putnam	100 00
"	Mrs. S. A. Wright...	20 00
"	Seth Bemis, Newton.	50 00
"	Anonymous........	100 00
"	A Poor New Hampshire Boy	5 00
"	Anonymous, Middleborough	50 00
"	Edward Cruft.......	50 00
"	Mrs. S. Cabot, Brookline	100 00
"	Mrs. E. W. Forbush.	20 00
"	Dr. O. W. Holmes...	100 00
"	Dr. H. Richardson ..	25 00
"	Miss E. Richardson .	25 00
"	Wm. B. Bradford ...	50 00
"	Messrs. Faulkner, Kimball & Co......	500 00
"	Wellington Brothers, East Cambridge...	50 00
"	Elisha Atkins.......	100 00
"	Master Edwin F. Atkins	10 00
"	James L. Little......	250 00
"	Wm. Munroe	200 00
"	Dr. Edward Reynolds	50 00
"	Miss Mason........	50 00
"	Miss S. L. Mason....	25 00
"	Hon. P. Sprague	30 00
"	Mrs. J. M..:......	10 00
"	Samuel A. Way.....	100 00
"	J. S. Barstow.......	100 00
"	George M. Soule....	100 00
"	C. A. Cummings....	25 00
"	C. F. Hovey & Co...	500 00
"	Wm. P. Mason......	200 00
"	Mrs. Daniel Denny..	100 00
"	Dr. W. R. Lawrence.	100 00
"	Joseph H. Billings...	50 00
"	Fees of referees.....	30 00
"	Amherst, by the hands of Col. W. S. Clark	250 00
	Carried up.....	$24,527 00

March 1,	Brought up.......	$24,527 00
"	E. S................	20 00
"	Milton Hill	10 00
"	C. and J., two poor young men	4 00
"	Benjamin R. Gilbert.	50 00
"	Alexander Beal, Dorchester	25 00
"	B. D. Emerson, Jamaica Plain	100 00
"	Ezra Abbot, Cambridge	20 00
"	A lady in Cambridge	20 00
"	John Bertram, Salem	200 00
"	Hon. R. H. Dana, jr..	30 00
"	Geo. W. Wheelright	50 00
"	Forest Hill St., Roxbury	5 00
"	Miss C. H. Wild	25 00
"	Weld Farm, West Roxbury	80 00
"	Edward Atkinson ...	50 00
"	D. W. Salisbury	100 00
"	Burr Brothers & Co.	200 00
"	Henry L. Pierce, Dorchester............	100 00
"	Francis Cabot	25 00
"	Arthur Searle.......	20 00
"	C. K...............	10 00
"	A. H...............	5 00
"	Messrs. Claflin, Saville & Co............	100 00
"	Eaton, Cumings & Co.	100 00
"	Cambridge..........	50 00
"	Francis Williams, Quincy	100 00
"	Mrs. E. H. D........	25 00
March 2,	Henry Williams.....	25 00
"	A school-girl's monthly allowance	1 00
"	Uncle Ben, Savin Hill	10 00
"	A friend in Cambridge	10 00
"	Elbridge Torrey......	10 00
"	Mrs. James Lawrence	200 00
"	Professor Asa Gray, Cambridge.........	20 00
"	L. Grozelier........	10 00
"	C. W. Clark........	25 00
"	E.................	3 00
"	A friend in Roxbury.	6 00
"	A friend............	10 00
"	Anonymous, by the hands of J. I. Bowditch	100 00
"	Mrs. N. I. Bowditch.	500 00
".	J. Ingersoll Bowditch	200 00
"	Mrs. J. I. Bowditch..	100 00
"	Wm. Claflin........	200 00
"	Hon. Seth Ames....	50 00
"	S. C. Thwing.......	100 00
	Carried over....	$27,631 00

March 2, Brought over	$27,631 00
" Rev. Dr. Ellis & Mrs. Ellis, Charlestown.	100 00
" Mrs. H. B. Rogers...	100 00
" William Read & Son.	100 00
" Anonymous.........	50 00
" Master Jas. Lawrence, jr................	2 00
" Anonymous, in Mount Vernon Street.....	15 00
" D. P. Ives..........	100 00
" M. L. C.............	100 00
" I. E. Piper..........	5 00
" Rev. Dr. Bartol.....	50 00
" Leverett Saltonstall..	100 00
" Ariel Low & Co.....	100 00
" H. H. Hunnewell....	300 00
" Wm. Gray, jr........	250 00
" Mrs. S. P. Miles, Brattleboro...........	50 00
" Rev. R. Ellis, second donation..........	10 00
" A small boy........	1 00
" Sam'l Frothingham..	50 00
" Sam'l Frothingham, jr................	50 00
" Dr. Henry ·Bartlett, Roxbury	50 00
" I..................	5 00
" S. G. Snelling.......	50 00
" Lindsley, Shaw & Co.	100 00
" Henry Wainwright..	100 00
" From one who has very little of this world's goods.....	2 00
" Howland, Hinckley & Co.	50 00
" J. G. Kidder........	100 00
" John A. Blanchard..	100 00
" Naylor & Co........	300 00
" Sewall, Day & Co....	100 00
" J. Field	200 00
" Chas. H. Coffin, Newburyport	100 00
" Mrs. M.............	28 00
" F..................	100 00
" Charles B. Poor.....	25 00
" " See Acts xx. 35 "..	10 00
" J. W. Paige........	100 00
March 3, J. F. B. Marshall....	50 00
" Miss Harriet S. Hayward.............	100 00
" Lemuel Shaw.......	50 00
" E. W. B............	5 00
" A. B. Almon, Salem.	30 00
" George H. Gray and Danforth	200 00
" Hon. Albert Fearing.	100 00
" Hon. Rob't C. Winthrop	50 00
Carried up......$31,269 00	

March 3, Brought up.......	$31,269 00
" George D. Welles....	50 00
" Oliver Ditson.......	100 00
" E. B. Phillips.......	25 00
" Mrs. R. G. Shaw....	200 00
" Miss Louisa Shaw...	25 00
" Jona. French, Roxbury	100 00
" Mrs. James Sturgis..	50 00
" John G. Tappan.....	100 00
" Charles F. Bradford, Roxbury.........	50 00
" Charles K. Cobb	50 00
" George J. Fiske.....	100 00
" Homer Bartlett	50 00
" " Homo Sum "......	8 00
" James W. Sever.....	50 00
" Hon. Edward Brooks	200 00
" Francis Brooks	100 00
" Joseph E. Worcester, Cambridge	100 00
" A New England Sister to her brave and suffering young sisters in E. Tennessee	5 00
" George Gardner.....	300 00
" E. M. and E. A. C...	10 00
" Charles Heath	50 00
" Mrs. Charles Heath..	50 00
" Miss E. Parsons.....	50 00
" The contents of a savings-bank from two little boys	2 00
" S. Willard & Son....	100 00
" J. C. W.............	25 00
" Larkin, Stackpole & Co..............	100 00
" A Book-keeper......	10 00
" Edward S. Philbrick.	100 00
" Beacon Hill........	15 00
" Fishers & Chapin....	100 00
" From R.............	1 00
" From 509...........	5 00
" Samuel May........	200 00
" John J. May........	100 00
" Nath'l Winsor & Son	100 00
" William S. Eaton...	50 00
" Thomas Groom.....	50 00
" Maguire & Campbell.	50 00
" L. A. Shattuck......	50 00
" Reuben A. Richards.	50 00
" Franklin King.......	50 00
" From Minnie & Nelly	10 00
" T. E. M............	5 00
" Francis Bacon.......	100 00
" William Ropes......	100 00
" E. L...............	10 00
" W. H. R............	5 00
" Isaac Thacher.......	100 00
" Elizabeth J. Stone...	10 00
Carried over....$ 34,590 00	

March 3,	Brought over	$34,590 00
"	David W. Hodgdon..	50 00
"	D. A. Dwight & Co..	100 00
"	William Perkins....	100 00
"	Robert S. Perkins...	50 00
"	J. W. P. Abbott, Westford.....	25 00
"	William Raymond...	10 00
March 4,	Otis Daniel.........	200 00
"	F. Snow & Co.......	100 00
"	Edward O. Banvard, Calais, Maine	50 00
"	The Misses Snow, Roxbury	200 00
"	D. C., Calais, Maine.	5 00
"	M................	25 00
"	C. T...............	5 00
"	Chief Justice Bigelow	50 00
"	Sidney Homer......	100 00
"	Mrs. H. S...........	15 00
"	Hon. George Morey.	50 00
"	Mrs. Sarah Johnson.	50 00
"	R. E. Robbins.......	250 00
"	A Physician, who promises the same every Saturday for five weeks........	10 00
"	Dane, Dana & Co....	100 00
"	Avon Place.........	30 00
"	Little, Brown & Co..	200 00
"	Capt. Arthur H.Clark	20 00
"	Benjamin C. Clark..	20 00
"	Miss Donnison, Cambridge...........	50 00
"	Hon. James Savage..	200 00
"	Prof. W. B. Rogers..	25 00
"	William Sprague....	100 00
"	Thos. G. Bradford...	25 00
"	Mr. and Mrs. Joseph S. Beal, Kingston..	50 00
"	George Draper, Hopedale, Mass........	50 00
"	Rev. Dr. George Putnam, Roxbury.....	100 00
"	Jona. B. Bright, Waltham	20 00
"	Andrew Warren, do..	5 00
"	O. W. Baker, do.....	5 00
"	Newell Sherman, do..	5 00
"	Marshall Smith, do..	3 00
"	Daniel French, do....	5 00
"	Dorus Clarke, do....	5 00
"	Dr. R. S. Warren, do.	5 00
"	Perez Smith, do.....	5 00
"	Rufus Stickney, do..	1 00
"	Cornelius Irish, do...	1 00
"	Phineas Upham, do..	5 00
"	Wm. Jewell, do.....	5 00
"	George Lawton, do..	10 00
"	John Roberts, do...	10 00
	Carried up	$37,095 00

March 4,	Brought up.......	$37,095 00
"	C. L. Mosely, Waltham.............	5 00
"	Jarvis Lewis, do.....	2 00
"	Wm. E. Allen, do....	3 00
"	Federalist...........	30 00
"	Mrs. David Sears....	100 00
"	C. L. F. R.	50 00
"	Dr. Wm. W. Morland	20 00
"	In a blank envelope..	20 00
"	Chandler & Co.......	100 00
"	J. A. & W. Bird & Co.	50 00
"	Seth Turner, Randolph.............	50 00
"	'68.................	1 00
"	Walter Channing, M. D................	100 00
"	Samuel B. Pierce ...	50 00
"	A Webfoot..........	10 00
"	A Widow	20 00
"	Benj. Thaxter.......	50 00
"	Anonymous, by the hands of J. I. Bowditch...........	150 00
"	W. S. Appleton.....	100 00
"	Daniel N. Spooner...	100 00
"	George F. Parkman .	200 00
"	William Beals.......	100 00
"	Francis B. Hayes....	100 00
"	N. B. Gibbs.........	100 00
"	Henry B. Rogers....	500 00
"	John A. Dodd & Co..	100 00
"	A friend............	5 00
"	J. W. Wheelwright..	50 00
"	E. A. Boardman	30 00
"	Dr. G. C. Shattuck..	100 00
"	C. C. Gilbert........	50 00
"	David W. Williams, Roxbury	100 00
"	Charles Emery	20 00
March 5,	Geo. C. Lord, Newton	100 00
"	Charles H. Lord, do..	100 00
"	Edward W. Lord, do.	28 00
"	H. Williams, do.	10 00
"	Nash,Spaulding & Co.	300 00
"	A. F. — Salem......	5 00
"	F. H. M............	5 00
"	Hon. Emory Washburn.............	50 00
"	James Hayward.....	100 00
"	From Longwood	5 00
"	S. W. Rodman......	50 00
"	Anonymous.........	10 00
"	John Cormerais.....	25 00
"	Dr. John Dean......	20 00
"	J. J. Dixwell........	50 00
"	Mrs. Anna Parker...	50 00
"	Grant, Warren & Co.	300 00
"	George R. Russell...	200 00
"	Mrs. F. C. Paine	25 00
	Carried over....	$40,994 00

March 5,	Brought over....	$40,994 00
"	Gardner, Dexter & Co...............	100 00
"	James Read........	100 00
"	Mrs. James Read...	100 00
"	Augustine Heard...	100 00
"	A little boy, 6 years old, his own money	1 00
"	Ellice	30 00
"	Charles W. Parker.	100 00
"	Joshua Stetson.....	100 00
"	Hon. S. Williston, E. Hampton	100 00
"	Anonymous, proc'ds of the sale of unnecessary silver plate	12 00
"	E. F. Waters.......	25 00
"	The Misses Newman	200 00
"	C. C. Perkins, Italy	100 00
"	Curtis & Co........	100 00
"	Lizzie Leland......	20 00
"	Edward Motley	50 00
"	From three friends .	85 00
"	D. B. Flint	50 00
"	Charles L. Young..	50 00
"	Waldo Maynard....	50 00
"	Francis Bassett.....	100 00
"	Mrs. W. C. Codman	50 00
"	Thomas Worcester.	100 00
"	Aunt Betsey.......	5 00
"	Dr. Le Baron Russell	50 00
"	David B. Sewall, Fryeburg, Me. ...	6 00
"	Santuit River, Cotuit	5 00
March 7,	A. A. Lawrence, jr., Brookline........	50 00
"	S. W. Vinson, clerk	5 00
"	T. Lee.............	100 00
"	John H. Thorndike.	50 00
"	Mrs. E. Miller and Charles E. Miller, Quincy	100 00
"	Mrs. J. G. Howard, South Braintree..	10 00
"	Samuel Gilbert, Boston	50 00
"	Samuel Gilbert, jr., Dorchester	50 00
"	George W. Harding, do...............	100 00
"	W. C. Harding, Roxbury	100 00
"	A lady............	10 00
"	Officers and men of the 44th Regiment Massachusetts Volunteers *	1000 00
	Carried up......	$44,408 00

* The very liberal donation of the 44th

March 7,	Brought up......	$44,408 00
"	Dana, Farrar & Hyde	200 00
"	Crab Apple........	5 00
"	Foster & Taylor....	200 00
"	Otis Norcross	100 00
"	His Honor, F. W. Lincoln, Jr., Mayor	50,00
"	Hon. J. Z. Goodrich	500 00
"	Bigelow, Brothers & Kennard	100 00
"	A lady	10 00
"	Mrs. N. H. Emmons	100 00
"	A friend in Cambridge...........	20 00
"	G. M., Norfolk County..........	10 00
March 8,	A dictate of conscience for the suffering Loyalists of East Tennessee...	200 00
"	A friend to the good cause...........	20 00
"	Edward D. Peters & Co...............	300 00
"	Samuel Atherton...	50 00
"	A. W. S...........	50 00
"	Anonymous, from Worcester.......	5 00
"	Eben C. Stanwood & Co.	100 00
"	Brewster, Sweet & Co...............	100 00
"	George N. Hastings, (12 years) E. Cambridge...........	1 00
"	Walter H. Whitney, (10 years) E. Cambridge...........	1 00
	Carried over..	$46,530 00

Regiment was accompanied by the following letter: —

"BOSTON, *March* 5, 1864.

" HON. EDWARD EVERETT —

" Dear Sir: Through the liberality of their fellow-citizens, the Regiment which I have the honor to command, received a Regimental Fund of $5000. A portion of this money has been applied to the use of the Regiment, — a portion I retain for further need of the Regiment. Upon consultation with Wm. Gray, Esq., Treasurer of the fund, and with my field officers, and feeling sure that it will meet the approval of the original donors, I have decided to devote $1000 to the relief of the suffering loyalists of East Tennessee, which please accept in behalf of the men and officers of the 44th Regt. M. V. M.

" I am, sir, your obedient servant,
" FRANCIS L. LEE,
" Col. 44th Regt. M. V. M."

March 8, Brought over....$46,530 00
" William Brigham... 50 00
" Robert B. Storer ... 50 00
" " Somebody "...... 50 00
" W. P. Pierce....... 200 00
" P. Anderson, Lowell 25 00
" Jas. W. Walworth.. 100 00
" Isaac Livermore.... 50 00
" An old lady....... 50 00
" O. H. Sampson..... 25 00
" William A. Bangs.. 25 00
" J. Dixwell Thomp-
      son............. 25 00

The following most liberal contributions to the fund, to the amount of $4,773, were obtained in Franklin St. and vicinity, through the energetic and disinterested coöperation of Mr. George H. Braman, of No. 51 Franklin St. : —

March 8, Jordan, Marsh & Co. 500 00
" Friend of the Coun-
      try.............. 500 00
" Wilson, Hamilton &
      Co............. 250 00
" J. C. Burrage & Co. 250 00
" Hogg, Brown & Tay-
      lor............. 250 00
" Parker, Wilder & Co. 240 00
" Denny, Rice & Co.. 300 00
" Washburn, Welch &
      Carr............. 200 00
" Haughton, Sawyer &
      Co............. 200 00
" Almy, Patterson &
      Co............. 200 00
" Pierce, Bros. & Co.. 100 00
" King, Goodridge &
      Co............. 100 00
" Sweetzer, Swan &
      Blodget.......... 100 00
" Burrage, Bros. & Co. 100 00
" George S. Winslow
      & Co........... 100 00
" Wilkinson, Lamb &
      Co............. 100 00
" J. C. Converse & Co. 100 00
" Anderson, Heath &
      Co............. 100 00
" Hill, Danforth & Co. 100 00
" Ordway, Tebbetts &
      Co............. 100 00
" John C. Morse & Co. 50 00
" Allen, Lane & Co... 50 00
" Mrs. Isaac Fenno... 50 00
" Thayer, Badger &
      Plimpton........ 50 00
" Stone, Wood & Co.. 50 00
" Woodman, Horse-
      well & Co........ 50 00

Carried up.....$51,370 00

March 8, Brought up......$51,870 00
" C. Curry.......... 50 00
" H. E. Wright & Co.. 50 00
" F. A. Hawley & Co. 50 00
" Bliss, Whiting, Pierce
      & McKenna...... 50 00
" Clerks at Jordan,
      Marsh & Co...... 82 00
" Clerks at Ordway,
      Tebbetts & Co.... 31 00
" Whitney, Crain &
      Marr........... 25 00
" Gross, Daniels & Co. 25 00
" Whitten, Burdett &
      Young.......... 25 00
" Washburn, Foque &
      Co.............. 25 00
" Sargent, Brothers &
      Co.............. 25 00
" Lewis Coleman & Co. 25 00
" Geo. W. Simmons &
      Co.............. 25 00
" F. F. Wheelock &
      Co.............. 20 00
" N. H. Clark........ 20 00
" Devonshire Street.. 10 00
" George Alden...... 5 00

March 9, No. 58 Milk Street.. 25 00
" Thomas B. Wales.. 100 00
" Levi Bartlett & Co.. 100 00
" Hon. Stephen Salis-
      bury, Worcester.. 300 00
" George C. Richard-
      son............. 200 00
" H................. 25 00
" J. P. Thorndike.... 100 00
" A lady in Berk-
      shire............ 10 00
" Edward N. Perkins,
      Jamaica Plain ... 50 00
" Keene............. 10 00
" Edward S. Tobey... 200 00
" Anonymous, by the
      hand of E. S. To-
      bey 25 00
" Ex-Gov'nor Lincoln 100 00
" Gardner Brewer &
      Co.............. 200 00
" Geo. P. Hayward &
      Co.............. 25 00
" J. C. B., Lexington. 25 00
" William Dall....... 100 00
" Two ladies in Rox-
      bury 20 00
" Miss Henrietta Sar-
      gent 20 00
" Israel Whitney..... 25 00
" Nathan Matthews .. 100 00

Carried over...$53,673 00

March 9, Brought over....	$53,673 00	
Walter H. Whitney, second donation..	1 00	
" M. D.............	10 00	
" Proceeds of Mr. Siddons's reading....	100 00	
March 10, Mrs. E. D. H......	5 00	
" Rev. Geo. M. Rice, Westford........	5 00	
" Anonymous........	100 00	
" B.S., 29 Bowdoin St.	25 00	
" Citizens of Hallowell, Me., per Justin E. Smith........	203 00	
" John H. Sturgis....	50 00	
" J. P. Preston.......	100 00	
" William F. Matchett	25 00	
" Lucretia A. R., Baltimore, Md.......	5 00	
" Drop in the bucket.	5 00	
" Soldiers' Aid Soc'ty, Winthrop, by the hand of Mrs. J. C. Hall, Treasurer ..	50 00	
" Samuel G. Ward...	100 00	
" Mrs. T. W. Ward..	100 00	
" Benj. Abbott.......	25 00	
" W................	10 00	
" Mrs. H...........	100 00	
" Mrs. Nathan Appleton.............	100 00	
" Hon.Richard Fletcher.........	100 00	
" H. E. J...........	5 00	
" Mrs. Judge Putnam *.........	30 00	
" J. M. Forbes.....:..	250 00	
" Hon. James Arnold, New Bedford.....	500 00	
" E. S. Dixwell......	20 00	
" Hon. David Sears..	150 00	
" A Teacher........	2 00	

The following sums were remitted by Rev. C. H. Brigham, being, with the exception of the donation of Mr. Baylies, contributed by the First Congregational Church in Taunton : †

Samuel B. King............	100 00
Theodore Dean.............	100 00
Edmund Baylies	100 00
Mrs. George A. Crocker	50 00
Timothy Gordon...........	50 00

Carried up.... $56,249 00

* This venerable lady contributed by her needle-work over a hundred dollars to the fair of the Sanitary Commission.
† The liberal contribution from the First Congregational Society in Taunton was announced in a letter from its pastor,

Brought up.....	$56,249 00
Francis B. Dean............	50 00
Joseph Dean................	50 00
Artemas Briggs	50 00
Sylvanus N. Staples.........	50 00
Allen Presbrey..............	25 00
Charles R. Atwood..........	25 00
Charles H. Brigham	25 00
Enoch Robinson.............	25 00
William Brewster	25 00
Le Baron B. Church.........	25 00
Jesse Hartshorn.............	20 00
A. King Williams	20 00
James Henry Sproat.........	20 00
Nathan A Skinner...........	20 00
Charles H. Brigham........	20 00
Samuel O. Dunbar	10 00
Henry C. Perry.............	10 00
Edwin Keith................	10 00
C. W. Sproat and W. E. Fuller	7 00
Billings T. Presbrey.........	5 00
James P. Ellis..............	5 00
Mrs. G. L. Macomber........	5 00
Wm. T. Crandell.............	2 00
Mrs. G. C. Converse........	1 00

March 10, Mrs. J. W........		25 00
" Chas. Hickling, Roxbury		50 00
" A "mite-y man of Salem".........		10 00
" Lawton............		10 00
" Two ladies		22 00
" D. W. H...........		25 00
" Hartley, Lord & Co.		100 00
" George T. Rice, Worcester		100 00
March 11, A Son of Massachusetts,Charlestown, N. H.		5 00
" F. Nickerson & Co..		100 00
" Rev. Dr. S. K. Lothrop.............		10 00

Carried over... $57,211 00

Rev. Charles H. Brigham, from which, without his permission, I venture to make an extract, for the sake of showing the noble spirit that animates that community : —

"TAUNTON, *March 9th*, 1864.

"DEAR SIR, — On Sunday last, according to the suggestion of your circular address, I called the attention of my people, in a special sermon, to the sufferings of the Patriots in East Tennessee, and asked for their offerings. In two days I have received $740, which will probably become $800 or $900, as the smaller subscriptions come in. This is from my own congregation."

March 11,	Brought over....	$57,211 00
"	M. W.	5 00
"	Citizens of Amherst, N. H., by the hands of B. B. David	282 00
"	Master Henry Eliot Babcock	5 00
"	James C. Ward, Northampton	25 00
"	P. Holmes, Kingston	100 00
"	Wm. S. Adams, do..	100.00
"	Sabin & Page	30 00
"	Mrs. D. C——, Lancaster, Mass.	10 00
"	Milton Railway	2 00
"	A friend	5 00
"	Mrs. J. Gardner	50 00
"	"Brighton"	100 00
"	Wm. Knowlton, Upton	100 00
"	Franklin Haven	100 00
"	Proprietors of the "Christian Examiner"	20 00
"	George Allen	50 00
"	Boston Boy, — the same who gave the donation on the 12th Feb.	10 00
"	Mrs. Abbott	25 00
"	Tremont	50 00
"	Peter Smith, Andover, Mass.	100 00
"	Two sisters, M. & A.	5 00
March 12,	Edwin Upton	50 00
"	Francis Draper, Cambridge	50 00
"	Alpheus Hardy & Co.	100 00
"	Webster & Co.	100 00
"	Sampson Reed	50 00
"	A. H.	20 00
"	Reed, Cutler & Co.	100 00
"	Anonymous	25 00
"	E. B. Welch	50 00
"	The Centre Church in Haverhill, by the hand of Rev. Mr. Munger	286 00
"	D. H. B.	8 00
"	Anonymous	40 00
"	E. H.	25 00
"	Edward Warren, M. D., Newton Lower Falls	25 00
"	Physician's second week's donation	10 00
"	Currier & Greeley	100 00
"	A friend	10 00
	Carried up	$59,434 00

	Brought up....	$59,434 00
March 12,	Mrs. J. M. Codman, Brookline	50 00
"	W. T.	5 00
"	First Church in Taunton, additional	65 00
March 14,	A.	5 00
"	Rev. Dr. C. A. Bartol, a second donation of	50 00
"	Mrs. Nancy White	50 00
"	A school-boy	1 00
"	George Hews	25 00
"	C. Ellis, M. D.	50 00
"	E. H. Eldredge	100 00
"	Rolfe Eldredge	50 00
"	The venerable President Quincy	100 00
"	Anonymous	25 00
"	Ditto	25 00
"	Wm. M. Byrnes	20 00
"	G. Rogers	20 00
"	Isaac F Dobson	100 00
"	Cash	20 00
"	J. W. B.	50 00
"	S. E. P.	50 00
"	R. D. R.	50 00
"	F. C.	50 00
"	W. T. G.	50 00
"	P. S. C.	25 00
"	Cash	20 00
"	W. P., jr.	25 00
"	Francis Peabody	100 00
"	Cash	5 00
"	W. Amory	100 00
"	Cash	25 00
"	J. P. Gardner	50 00
"	J. D. Bates	50 00
"	Cash	25 00
"	Ditto	25 00
"	Ditto	100 00
"	G. M. Barnard	100 00
"	T. Quincy Browne	50 00
"	Iasigi, Goddard & Co.	300 00
"	Miss M. G. Loring	50 00
"	O	2 00
"	Waldo Flint	50 00
"	A friend to the suffering	10 00
"	A little girl	1 00
"	Anonymous	10 00
"	Mrs. Tyler Bigelow, Watertown	100 00
"	Mrs. Theodore Chase	50 00
March 15,	Anonymous	10 00
"	A lady of Bridgewater	5 00
"	A. Bummer, Cambridge	5 00
"	W. P. H., Cambridge	1 00
	Carried over...	$61,739 00

Brought over....		$61,739 00
March 15, Mary Leary, Halifax, N. S., now of West Newton		2 00
"	Dabney & Cunningham	50 00
"	From a lady in New Hampshire	100 00
"	A friend	25 00
"	G. Race..........	10 00
"	A poor old Duster..	2 00
"	J. R. H............	100 00
"	*Unitarian Society at Watertown....	415 60

The following sums were contributed by the pupils of Mr. T. Prentiss Allen's School, New Bedford † : —

M. Morris Howland.........	2 00
A. Thornton...............	2 00
E. Allen	2 00

Carried up..... $62,449 60

* The contribution from the Unitarian Society at Watertown was accompanied by the following letter from its Pastor: —

" WATERTOWN, 14th March, 1864.
" DEAR SIR, — Please devote the enclosed contribution from the Unitarian Society in this place to the sufferers in East Tennessee.

" This society is the representative of the old territorial parish, which was founded in the summer of 1630, with Rev. George Phillips for l'astor. But the original territory has shrunken to a little town, which was lately still further reduced by the scission of that portion now called Belmont, and the population of Watertown is now shared by four other societies besides our own.

" This contribution would have been larger if several of my parishioners had not already liberally subscribed at their places of business in Boston.

. " But accept the offering made at the close of service last Sunday, for brothers who suffer for their dear country's cause and glory.

" I am very respectfully yours,
[Signed]   " J. WEISS."

† The subscription paper at Mr. Allen's school had the following caption: —

· " The loyal boys of Massachusetts to the loyal boys of Tennessee send greeting: Having heard through Col. Taylor of the hardships and the privations that you have endured, while your fathers and our fathers have been struggling side by side, for the support of the Union cause and in defence of liberty, and feeling that, although remotely situated, we are broth-

Brought up	$62,449 60
Walter Clifford	2 00
G. Willis	2 00
R. Coggeshall...............	1 00
Arthur Clifford..............	2 00
P. R. Almy.................	1 00
B. R. Tucker	1 00
W. A. Bartlett..............	1 00
G. F. Tucker...............	1 00
A. G. Swift................	2 00
Horace Wood	1 00
E. C. Dubois...............	1 00
E. D. Antony...............	1 00
E. F. Tucker...............	1 00
W. Almy...................	2 00
C. Almy	1 00
J. Stoddard	10 00
E. Gordon..................	1 00
H. Swift...................	2 00
F. Swift...................	1 00'
Morgan Rotch...............	2 00
John B. Gerrish.............	2 00
James H. Harris	5 00
W. M. Thomp	1 00
H. B. Stone................	2 00
J. R. Chapman..............	2 00
Charles Almy...............	1 00
Henry A. Delano	1 00
D. L. Parker	1 00
J. Frank Perry..............	1 00
R. G. N. Swift..............	1 00
S. R. Potter...............	3 00
J. C. Tripp................	1 00
Willard Nye, jr..............	1 00
J. N. Faulkner..............	2 00
C. N. Swift................	1 00'
The Master of the School	8 00'

March 15, Jona. Howland, New Bedford.........		50 00
"	Capt. Latham Croos, do.	50 00
"	W. R. Austin, Dorchester	25 00
"	From a boy, his own money	4 00
"	A little girl, L. S...	3 00

Carried over $62,650 60

ers and have a united interest in the prosperity of our glorious country, we wish to manifest to you our sympathy; and as we have been prosperous while you have been suffering, we wish to send you a trifle from our abundance. Accept then these contributions from our own private stores, and be assured we are happy to do our part toward relieving your wants and encouraging you to hold out, until better days shall come, as we hope they will soon come to you."

8

	Brought over....	$62,650 60
March 15,	Congregational Ch. in Shrewsb'y, from the Pastor, Rev. Wm. McGinley...	53 50
"	E. H.	1 00
"	P. A. Gay	50 00
"	N. G. Manson	50 00
"	First Evangelical Cong'ational Ch. in Cambridgeport.	234 92
March 16,	A. L.	5 00
"	Sympathizer	5 00
"	Joseph Willard	25 00
"	J. K. P.	5 00
"	Two ladies of Northborough	20 00
"	Mrs. Deborah Powers, Lansinb'rg, N. Y., remitted by D. Powers & Sons	500 00
"	Rev. S. M. Worcester, Salem	10 00
"	Sophy Hayes	20 00
"	Hon. Jno. H. Clifford, New Bedford	100 00
"	A lady	10 00
"	Edward Page	50 00
"	W. C. Cabot	25 00
"	W. & R.	100 00
"	Mrs. Gam'l Bradford	50 00
"	George P. Bradford.	5 00
"	Samuel May, jr., Leicester	10 00
"	William B. Howes, Salem	100 00
"	A. C.	50 00
"	Amos Cummings	50 00
"	Two ladies in Cambridge	10 00
"	F. Vinton	5 00
March 17,	A Little Help	20 00
"	Claire A. L. Rice, Danvers Centre	5 00
"	F. & C.	2 00
"	Benj. B. Howard	50 00
"	Dorr, Parks & Co.	75 00
"	Citizens of Barnstable, forwarded by the Selectmen	338 00
"	Centre Street, Dorchester	20 00
"	J. H. Ward	100 00
"	Walter Aiken, Franklin, N. H.	10 00
"	N. P. G., a little girl	5 00
"	Cash	10 00
"	Osborn Howes	100 00
"	Miss M. E. Davis	10 00
"	Samuel T. Morse	25 00
	Carried up	$64,965 02

	Brought up....	$64,965 02
March 17,	J. Amory Davis, Dorchester	100 00
"	Edward Russell, do	50 00
"	H. I. Nazro, do	25 00
"	Seth Pettee, do	10 00
"	F. W. G. May, do	10 00
"	G. M. Weymouth, do	5 00
March 18,	Joseph A. White	50 00
"	P.	3 00
"	F. N. P.	5 00
"	Miss Arabella Rice, Portsmouth, N. H.	500 00
"	Benjamin Emerson, Pittsfield, N. H.	5 00
"	Ebenezer Collamore, Charlestown	50 00
"	A. B. Berlin	5 00
"	George May	100 00
"	Daniels, Kendall & Co.	100 00
"	From the friends of the sufferers in East Tennessee, Eastport, Me.	140 00
"	R. R. Endicott, Beverly	25 00
"	Ira E. Gray	20 00
March 19,	Proceeds of a vocal and instrumental concert at Plymouth	58 00
"	Q. H. D.'s	10 00
"	Oliver Prescott, New Bedford	50 00
"	Shawmut Sabbath School, by the hands of Wm. T. Shapleigh, Treasurer	119 77
"	The Physician's third week's subscription	10 00
"	S. A.	5 00
"	J. F.	5 00
"	P. D. W	5 00
"	B. B	5 00
"	J. D. R.	5 00
"	L. S. C.	5 00
"	J. A. T.	5 00
"	C. T. F.	5 00
"	R. M.	5 00
"	L. L.	5 00
"	S. H.	5 00
"	Wm. J. Rotch, New Bedford	100 00
"	Lyman Tiffany	100 00
"	J. P. Faulkner, North Billerica	25 00
	Carried over	$66,695 79

	Brought over....	$66,695 79
March 19,	John Perley, Salem.	80 00
"	Mrs. Persis K. Parkhurst, Templeton, Mass............	11 00
March 21,	Martha Hooper Lee	50 00
"	Miss Abigail Locke, Templeton.......	25 00
"	A friend	20 00
"	L. M.............	10 00
"	W. B. R...........	5 00
"	W. C. Tenney, Marlborough, Mass.............	50 00
"	D. Denny Rice, (aged 7 years) Roxbury........	1 21
"	L. and C. — two little boys — $1 50 each	3 00
"	John Bartlett, Cambridge...........	20 00
"	Citizens of Lexington, — chiefly the product of a collection taken in the First Parish Church, — by the hands of L. J. Livermore.......	281 25
"	R. B. Forbes	100 00
"	Proceeds of an amateur concert given March 19th, at Messrs. Chickering's Rooms which were generously offered for the occasion, by the hands of Dr. D. D. Slade	600 00
"	Collection taken in the First Church in Abington, remitted by Rev. F. R. Abbe........	70 00
"	Collection taken in the Shepard Congregational Society, Cambridge, remitted by S. T. Farwell	165 50
"	Additional from the 1st Evang. Congregational Ch. at Cambridgeport. ..	12 00
"	George H. Kuhn ...	100 00
"	S. F. Jenkins	100 00
"	A. S. Woodworth .	25 00
March 22,	Teachers and pupils of the Berkshire Family School, at	

Carried up.... $68,374 75

	Brought up......	$68,374 75
	Stockbridge, from the Principal, Ferdinand Hoffman..	67 50
March 22,	W. Chadbourne ...	100 00
"	A few Citizens of Danvers	178 00
"	AllenGannett, Lynnfield	2 00
"	Proceeds of a dramatic exhibition and concert given by the young ladies and gentlemen connected with the Mayflower Division, No. 33, S. of T. of Provincetown, Mass., remitted by James Gifford	100 00
"	E.................	5 00
"	Several young ladies	67 00
"	Elmer Townsend ..	50 00
"	Collection taken at Trinity Church on Sunday last, (including a check for $200, from H. W. Sargent, Esq., of the State of New York), by the hands of the Senior Warden of the Church	385 00
"	Shepard Congregational Society of Cambridge, additional	30 00
	"A Graft of the Brokers' Board ".......	50 00
"	Anonymous	5 00
"	Jonathan Bourne, jr. New Bedford.....	100 00
"	E. J..............	20 00
"	A little girl........	5 00
"	Collection taken in the First Congregational Society of Royalston, remitted by Hon. George Whitney	60 00
"	Citizens of Plymouth, through Andrew L. Russell, Esq. (this is in addition to the $58 received from Plymouth on the 19th, making in all $700)	642 00

Carried over.... $70,241 25

Brought over....$70,241 25	
March 22, From the ladies and gentle'n of Brookline, remitted by J. Murray Howe, Esq.	437 00
" Collections made at the Unitarian, Orthodox, and Universalist Societies in W. Cambridge, — in addition to $200 from J. Field and $100 from G. H. Gray, previously acknowledged	466 56
" *George F. Bartlett, New Bedford, six Eng. sovereigns, valued at........	43 00
March 23, Baptist Church in Sharon, by the hands of Mr. C. D. Hixon........	14 10
" A lady in Salem...	50 00
" Hon. Samuel Hooper, Washington..	200 00
" The family of C. Lord, Buckland, Mass...........	6 10
" C. M. Owen, Stockbridge...........	50 00
" Simeon N. Perry, Walpole, N. H....	30 00
" F. A. Sawyer......	50 00
Carried up $71,588 01	

* Mr. Bartlett's donation was accompanied by the following interesting letter to Mr. Everett: —

" NEW BEDFORD, *March* 21, 1864.
" DEAR SIR,— In response to Colonel Taylor's touching appeal, in behalf of our suffering loyal brethren in East Tennessee, I cheerfully part with the ONLY thing saved from the whaleship ' Lafayette,' burned by the Pirate ' Alabama,' April 15th, 1863, off Fernando de Noronha, and enclose the same to you herewith, viz. (6) Six English sovereigns, worth about forty-three dollars. Capt. Lewis was fortunately on shore with this gold to purchase stores, when Captain Semmes steamed around the island and burned his ship. I will regard it as a *forced* contribution from Capt. Semmes, in the name of the immortal Lafayette, who loved our country and its Father, and I am most happy in being able to make so worthy a bestowal of it.
" Yours respectfully,
[Signed.]   " GEORGE F. BARTLETT."

Brought up......$71,588 01	
March 23, Two " contrabands " by the hands of B. A. Nutt, Cambridge..........	5 00
March 24, " A Slice from our Daily Bread "....	5 00
" From Berlin and Longwood.......	75 00
" The Young Ladies Soldiers' Aid Society of Nashua, remitted by Miss Kate M. Thayer..	50 00
" Members of the Boston Corn Exchange..........	1130 00
" Geo. F. Hoar, Worcester...........	50 00
March 25, Benj. Snow, Fitchburg.............	50 00
" A few contributors in Stockbridge, received through Mr. Ferdinand Hoffman	50 00
" First Congregational Church and Society of Calais, Me., by Rev. Mr. S. H. Keeler..........	100 00
" Monument Church, South Deerfield, Mass., by Rev. David A. Strong.	10 00
" Proceeds of a morning concert in Mt. Vernon Street	260 00
" Citizens of Barnstable, — an additional contribution, through their Selectmen........	54 50
" Arthur Wilkinson..	100 00
" William Phillips & Son, New Bedford	75 00
" Mrs. Chs. K. Cobb..	50 00
" L. C. & E., Charlestown............	30 00
" Collection made in Rev. Dr. James W. Thompson's Church, at Jamaica Plain........	506 44
" *Collection made in	
Carried over $74,188 95	

* The donation from Chelsea was accompanied by the following letter: —

" CHELSEA, *March* 25, 1864.
" DEAR SIR,—We have been very much

Brought over....$74,188 95

Chelsea by three school-girls...... 45 00

March 26, Hon. Joseph Grinnell, New Bedford 100 00

"   H. C.............. 5 00

"   First Church in Boxford, by W. C. Kimball......... 107 25

"   Alex. Strong & Co. 100 00

"   Stone & Downer.... 100 00

"   Marlborough, collected by Rev. G. N. Anthony 304 65

"   M. H. G........... 5 00

"   Anonymous....... 1 00

"   II. A. A., in Memoriam, New Bedford 10 00

The   Physician's fourth week's subscription........ 10 00

"   Proceeds of Second Readings by Mr. Siddons and Miss Cameron......... 75 00

"   H. K. F., Charlestown............ 25 00

"   R. M. Mason, remitted from Paris 200 00

"   Anonymous, in addition to a former donation of $200.. 100 00

Carried up $75,376 85

interested in the patriotic people of East Tennessee, and not being able to aid them with money, we thought we perhaps might do so by devoting to them our leisure time, of which we had only our afternoons, as we are school-girls and have many lessons to learn. We have been from house to house in the little town of Chelsea, which is far from rich, with a subscription paper, asking from each person the small sum of ten or fifteen cents. The enclosed is the result of our efforts. It might be a comforting thought to the suffering Tennesseeans if they could know how generous and interested even the poorest people have been in their cause. One poor old woman gave all the money she had (seven cents) with the earnest wish that it was a great deal more, and that it might also do a little good.

" Hoping that this may bring half as much comfort to some hungry Tennesseean as we have had pleasure in collecting it, we are,

" Very Respectfully,
" C. L. E.
" M. S. E.
" H. E. D."

8 *

Brought up $75,376 85

March 26, Hancock St. Church, Quincy, collected at a Prayer Meeting, by Rev. Mr. Thwing......... 26 15

"   E. H.............. 20 00

"   M. P. Grant....... 30 00

"   A sailor......... 5 00

"   Old North End..... 10 00

"   Proceeds of a little girls' fair near Plymouth Rock, remitted by B. W. Watson........ 13 00

"   E. P. Tileston, Dorchester.......... 100 00

"   Samuel Downer, do. 50 00

"   Joseph Dix, do..... 25 00

"   Lothrop & Moseley, do.............. 20 00

"   William W. Paige, do.............. 10 00

"   Daniel B. Stedman & Co. do........ 20 00

"   John Preston, do... 10 00

"   Wm. L. Clark, do.. 10 00

"   William B. Newbury, do. 10 00

"   Robt. L. Living, do. 5 00

"   Edward Jarvis, M. D., do........... 5 00

"   Alex. B.Wheeler, do. 5 00

"   Palmers & Bachelders,............. 100 00

"   Henry C. Rand, N. Cambridge 25 00

"   Collection taken in the Lawrence St. Congregational Ch., Lawrence, remitted by C. A. Colby........... 170 00

"   Collection taken in the Central Ch., Lynn, remitted by P. O. Knapp,.... 132 03

"   From the ladies and gentlemen of the private theatricals in   Chickering's Hall.............. 732 00

March 29, A friend.......... 50 00

"   Collections in Stockbridge, Massachusetts, made by R. B. Craig........ 111 00

"   Anonymous........ 8 00

Arpil 1, A Law Student at Cambridge, being

Carried over $77,079 03

	Brought over...	$77,079 03
	one half of all he has	2 00
April 1,	E. P. H.	10 00
"	Dr. Daniel Swan, Medford,	100 00
"	The Misses Welles..	200 00
"	Henry Edwards....	50 00
"	Elijah Bardwell, Hadley	5 00
"	Frederic Clapp	3 00
"	S. H. H.	5 00
"	Anonymous, Worcester	3 00
"	John Russell, Greenfield	100 00
"	Anonymous	1 00
"	Avon Place, second donation	20 00
"	F. Peirce & Co.	100 00
"	Mrs. Betsey S. Beal, Kingston	10 00
"	Congregational Ch. and Soc. at West Boylston, by Rev. J. H. Fitts	29 00
"	Amount given at St. Paul's Church on Easter Sunday...	50 00
"	Abraham Barker...	50 00
"	"Acts 11th chapter, 26th and 27th verses "	20 00
"	Collection made in the Greenville Baptist Church and Society, by Rev. N. P. Cooke,	44 56
"	Central Ch., Lynn, additional	10 00
"	George A. Newell..	50 00
"	Baptist Society in Royalston	25 00
"	Francis Chase, Royalston	1 00
"	General John S. Tyler	50 00
"	The Misses Baldwin, Dorchester	60 00
"	Master Charles L. B. Whitney, prize for excellence in declamation, Springfield, Mass.	3 00
"	William A. Wheeler, Dorchester	3 00
"	Congregational Ch. and Soc. at Mattapoisett, Mass...	42 32
"	A friend	5 00
	Carried up	$78,130 91

	Brought up....	$78,130 91
April 1,	H. B. Pearson	50 00
"	A Boston minister..	25 00
"	Edward C. Jones, New Bedford	100 00
"	"A little more help "	40 00
"	The following officers of the customs in Boston, $5 each, viz.:—R. C. Nichols, Wm. H. Gorham, N. H. Whitney, C. Judson, Jos. O. Cole, M. Eggleston, O. Nichols, P. F. Williston, Henry Loring, C. C. Woodman	50 00
April 2,	Collection at a meeting in Somerville	14 60
"	A. M. H., "all she had "	1 00
"	Arthur Searle	30 00
"	Samuel Johnson, his second contribution	100 00
"	A. S., Salem	20 00
"	To fulfil the intentions of one lately deceased, Salem..	10 00
"	From D. H. Rogan, Greenfield, Mass., being the contribution of an East Tennessee Refugee, and a few of his friends	12 00
"	H.	5 00
"	D. R. Greene, New Bedford	100 00
"	S. R. M.	50 00
"	Pupils in the Adams School at Dorchester	50 00
April 4,	"Unknown "	1 00
"	"A friend," with a poetical dedication	10 00
"	Mrs. R. P., of Salem	2 00
"	The Physician's fifth week's subscription	10 00
"	1st Trinitarian Congregational Ch. at Malden	35 00
"	S.	50 00
"	A. A. T.	30 00
"	The officers of the 20th Regiment of Mass. Volunteers,	
	Carried over	$78,926 51

	Brought over....$78,926 51	
	by the hands of Col. Francis W. Palfrey.........	125 00
April 4,	A Massachusetts family, now abroad	300 00
"	John B. Taft, Dorchester.........	20 00
"	Wm. H. Bangs, do.	15 00
"	Henry G. Denny, do.	10 00
"	Robert Johnson, do.	10 00
"	Charles Hunt, do.....	10 00
"	Thomas J. Allen, do.	10 00
"	A. H. Stevens, do...	10 00
"	R. & C. B. Minot, do.	5 00
"	Jno. G. Wood, do....	2 00
"	Enos How, do......	1 00
April 5,	Three little sisters..	3 00
"	Easter offering in the Church of the Disciples, Indiana Place, Boston....	241 43
"	From Bernardstown, Mass., by Alman Newcomb, Esq...	90 00
"	A friend	30 00
"	Mrs. Maria F. Sayles	500 00
"	The Teachers and Scholars of the Unitarian Sabbath School, Gloucester, Mass........	30 00
"	G. W. Messinger, Esq., being his salary for the year as Treasurer of First Church, Boston..	50 00
"	Saml. Frothingham, second donation ..	100 00
"	A friend in Stockbridge, additional.	10 00
April 6,	G. H.............	10 00
"	F. & A............	12 00
"	A friend in Newton Centre.........	10 00
"	Second Parish Sabbath School, Amherst............	20 00
"	Citizens of Auburn, Mass............	73 25
"	Mrs. McBurney Roxbury........	50 00
"	Collected by four little girls at Falmouth..........	15 45
April 7,	Congregational Parish in Southfield...	42 90
	*His Excellency, J. L. Motley, Jr.,	
	Carried up....$80,732 54	

* Mr. Motley, in the letter of 22d of

	Brought up......$80,732 54	
	Minister of the United States at Vienna.........	200 00
April 7,	R., from Providence, R. I.............	100 00
"	M. A. R., ...	3 00
"	"No Shirk,"	5 00
"	Frederick Taber, ..:	5 00
"	H. J. R.............	20 00
"	Collection at the Church in Housatonic, Mass., by Rev. Josiah Brewer, Pastor........	16 00
"	Collection in the Parish of St. Andrews, Hanover, by Rev. Samuel Cutler, Rector ...	46 00
"	"A Party Hack"..	1 50
"	Federalist	10 00
April 8,	A friend in Kingston, Mass........	20 00
"	Mrs. A., Worcester, Mass...........	6 00
"	Proceeds of a masquerade in Cambridge...........	150 00
"	F., Portsmouth, N. H...............	20 00
"	P. F., Beverly, Mass.	20 00
April 9,	From a "River town"..........	10 00
"	C.	10 00
"	Congregational Society of Milford, by Rev. A. A. Ellsworth, Pastor....	45 00
"	L.................	150 00
"	Rev. R. M. Hodges, Cambridge.......	100 00
"	Proceeds of an entertainment given un-	
	Carried over $81,670 04	

March, containing his liberal remittance, writes: —

"I enclose a check for $200, and I wish that it was in my power to send a much larger sum. When, in after days, the history of this unexampled insurrection against Liberty comes to be written, there will be few episodes more moving or more instructive than the record of those Tennesseeans who have so long sustained the Republic and its principles, amid such trial and at such sacrifices. Certainly it is no *charity* on our part to assist them, but a sacred duty, which I am sure that all will fulfil in proportion to their means."

Brought over....$81,670 04

der the auspices of
the Teachers' As-
sociation in Music
Hall, on the 24th
March............ 135 00

April 9, Proceeds of a Juve-
nile Concert at
Williams Hall.... 12 00

"   " Roxbury ".......   2 00

"   " Impecuniosus,"
Baltimore........   5 00

"   Hon. Ichabod Good-
win of Portsmouth,
from the estate of
the late Mrs. Char-
lotte Rice of that
city, and in pre-
sumed accordance
with what would
have been her
wishes 500 00

"   Teachers and Pupils
of the Unitarian
Sunday School at
Exeter, N. H..... 66 00

April 11, Joseph Lovejoy..... 25 00

"   C.   P.   Emmons,
Needham........ 25 00

"   A class in the Chest-
nut-street Congre-
gational Sabbath
School at Chel-
sea............. 25 00

"   W., Charlestown...   1 00

"   Proceeds of a fair
got up for the chil-
dren in East Ten-
nessee by eight
little girls at Ply-
mouth, viz. :—An-
na Y. Stoddard,
Mary Hodge, Liz-
zie C. Faulkner,
Abby W. Davis,
Joanna W. Davis,
NellieClark,Laura
Y. Loring, Edith
A. Andrews...... 80 00

"   Susan D. Rogers... 25 00

April 12, G. A. Bethune..... 50 00

"   Somerset Street.... 10 00

"   " Mariner," Newbu-
ryport..........   5 00

"   Missionary Ch. in
Lanesville, Glou-
cester, Mass., by
Rev. Thomas Mo-
rong 20 00

Carried up $82,656 04

Brought up......$82,656 04

April 12, Mrs. Henry Cutter,
Winchester...... 10 00

April 13, Anonymous, Yar-
mouth.......... 10 00

"   Miss S. B. Morton,
Milton Hill...... 50 00

"   Mrs. N. F. Safford,
Milton Hill...... 25 00

"   Hon. Samuel H.
Dale, Mayor of
Bangor.......... 25 00

"   Friends of East Ten-
essee in Nantucket 30 00

"   A Collection on Fast
Day at a Union
meeting of the
Baptist and Ortho-
dox churches in
Littleton........ 32 06

"   Isaac R. Gifford,
North Dartmouth 50 00

"   Lawrence St. Con-
gregational   Ch.,
Lawrence, addi-
tional 2 00

"   A friend, in Chelsea 100 00

"   Proceeds of two am-
ateur concerts at
Salem, given on
the 4th and 11th
instant, under the
auspices of Mr.
Manuel Fenollosa 650 00

April 14, " From   one who
keeps his money
as long as his con-
science will let
him "...........   5 00

"   L. and C., two little
boys.   Proceeds
of their fair in
Hancock Street...   5 10

"   Bessie L..........   2 00

"   Pupils and teacher
of the Eliot Sab-
bath School, New-
ton, Mass. 132 00

"   *Collection made in
the Sunday School
of the EliotChurch,
Newton, Mass., re-

Carried over $83,784 20

* Mr. Bacon, in transmitting the handsome donation of the Eliot Sunday School
writes, " We were stimulated to make
our collection as large as possible by the
liberal offer of our Sabbath School teacher to double whatever sum might be contributed by the school. The result was a
contribution of $132."

Brought over....$83,784 20
mitted, with the preceding, by Mr. George W. Bacon 127 50
April 14, "Alpine"......... 10 00
" Ladies' Aid Society, South Danvers... 50 00
" South Church, do. 52 33
" Baptist do. do. 5 55
" Methodist do. do. 20 00
" Unitarian do. do. 27 10
April 15, Anonymous........ 10 00
" W., Northampton.. 20 00
" C................. 5 00
" S................. 5 00
" Second Cong. Soc. in Nantucket, by Rev. J. K. Karcher 88 03
" Mass. Char. Fire Society............ 300 00
" Anonymous........ 20 00
" C. S............. 5 00
" S. H. Bourne, Kennebunk.......... 5 00
" Cora............. 25 00
April 16, Mrs. Mary Morton, Milton Hill...... 50 00
" Mrs. M. H. M. Thompson....... 25 00
" C. F. W........... 5 00
" Blodget & White... 100 00
" Thomas W. Mayhew, Westport Point............ 10 00
" Proceeds of tableaux at Jamaica Plains, by the hands of Miss Horton.......... 334 75
April 18, A dress-maker..... 5 00
" T. C.............. 10 00
" J., being net amount of three days' work 10 00
" S. Blackinton, North Adams.......... 100 00
" S. Johnson, do..... 50 00
" S. W. Brayton, do. 50 00
" Mrs. Mary B. Parkman............ 5 00
" M., second donation 100 00
" Chiefly raised by contributions in the several churches of Milbury, remitted by D. Atwood............ 150 00
" Turner Sargent, in addition to a former donation of the same amount.... 100 00

Carried up.....$85,664 46

Brought up......$85,664 46
April 18, Harry and Charlie.. 5 00
" The officers and crew of the United States ship Rattler, enclosed in a letter from Dr. Scollay Parker, A. A. Surgeon, dated off Hurricane Island, Mississippi River, 25th March, 1864............ 127 00
" T. Jefferson Coolidge............. 200 00
April 19, A Farmer of North Perry, Me....... 5 00
" C. D. Kellogg..... 20 00
" M. H., Rollinsford, N. H............. 25 00
" Citizens of Tyngsborough......... 23 00
" Collection made by three little girls in Concord, Mass. 50 00
" Citizens of Dennis, being the proceeds of an exhibition held there....... 37 00
" Anonymous....... 5 00
" Mrs. Henry Grew, a second donation of the same amount. 100 00
" Collection in the church of the Rev. Dr. Hill in Worcester, in addition to the very liberal contributions of individuals of the Society heretofore announced....... 222 00
" M., East Cambridge 10 00
April 20, First Congregational Church in New Marlboro', from Rev. C. C. Painter 40 00
" X. Y. Z........... 1 00
" Universalist Church in Shirley Village, by Rev. C. B. Lombard......... 41 00
" *Anonymous...... 500 00

Carried over ..$87,075 46

* This munificent donation was enclosed in a note in which the writer says:—
"I have stood in the fight many a day by the side of those East Tennesseeans, but I see there are yet other ways of doing one's duty towards them; so I add my contribution to their aid."

Brought over.....$87,075 46

April 21, Elias Keith, Rowe, Mass........... 6 00
"   S. P. Brown, Dover, Me..... .... 100 00
"   A few Citizens of York, Me., remitted by Mr. George Moody.......... 45 00
"   Proceeds of a little girls' fair in Dorchester last week : Fanny Downes, Anna Morse, Bertha Newbury, Lizzie Peirce, Lila Howard, and Emma Nazro, Committee.......... 200 45
April 22, "A Vermont Soldier on the Potomac". 1 15
"   A family on Dana Hill, Cambridge.. 15 00
"   E. P. N., Portsmouth, N. H.... 25 00
"   Proceeds of a young ladies' fair, held at No. 21 Boylston Place............1000 00
April 23, Citizens of Ipswich.. 385 00
Benjamin F. Clarke, Winchendon..... 5 00
"   A few ladies in Belmont, — collected by Miss Mack.... 57 00
"   Collection taken in Rev. Joshua Coit's Church at Brookfield, Mass....... 30 00
"   An American gentleman in Italy... 200 00
"   Aaron Roberts, Dover, N. H........ 10 00
"   W. J. H........... 2 00
"   A few individuals in North Parish, Portsmouth...... 150 00
"   "Dickens Dramatic Club," Cambridge 103 00
April 24, From a friend, by J. J. M.......... 50 00
"   First Baptist Church in Dorchester, by Rev. Mr. Barrows 17 50
"   C. & J. A.......... 10 00
"   "In Memoriam," F. C. L. and F. S. M. 40 00
"   F. A. E........... 30 00
"   Members of the M. E. Church in Dor-

Carried up.....$89,557 56

Brought up $89,557 56
chester, by Rev. C. S. Rogers..... 35 00
April 24. Collection in the Congregational Church at South Reading........ 72 18
"   Social gathering at do. 46 00
Collection in the Unitarian Church in North Chelsea, Rev. W. O. Moseley, Pastor....... 84 00
"   Collection at the Crombie Street Church and Society at Salem, by Henry J. Pratt... 73 47
"   Penny contributions of the Mt. Vernon Sabbath School for one month, by Warren L. Tower, Treasurer........ 25 00
"   Lafayette Burr, — formerly a resident at the South 50 00
"   Miss Wales, — in addition to a previous contribution of $300, before reported 200 00
April 26, Collection taken at the Church of the Unity at Worcester, Rev. Mr. Shippen, Pastor,..... 158 00
"   Collection taken at the Congregational Church at Wenham, Rev. J. S. Sewall, Pastor... 29 00
"   Unitarian Sunday School at Quincy, L. P. Forbush, Superintendent... 252 10
April 27, Chas. K. Cobb, in addition to two former donations of same amount..... 50 00
"   Collected in New Bedford, by Master Willie Howland, who was prevented from getting more by illness.. 3 50
"   Collection at the Dorchester Village Church. Rev. Mr. Rich, Pastor...... 53 25

Carried over... $90,639 01

Brought over ...$90,639 01		
April 27, Collection at the Church of the Third Religious Society of Dorchester, Rev. I. J. Mumford, Pastor..............	100 00	
" * Collection taken at the First Church, Dorchester, Rev. Mr. Hall, Pastor..	272 50	
" Collection at the First Independent Methodist Church, Dorchester, Rev. Mr. Pettee, Pastor	13 35	
" Cyrus Brewer, Dorchester..........	10 00	
" Miss M. H. Hooper, Dorchester.......	5 00	
" J. H. B. Lang, Dorchester..........	20 00	
" "A friend" by J. J. M., Dorchester	20 00	
" C. P. Lewis, do.	15 00	
" Wm. Hendry, do.	10 00	
" D. C. Holden, do.	5 00	
" G. T. Stoddard, do.	2 00	
April 28, Anonymous, from Worcester........	2 00	
" Profit on 700 shares Sutton Copper Co.	10 00	

Carried up $91,123 86

* The contributions from Dorchester were transmitted in the following noble letter from the Selectmen: —

DORCHESTER, *April* 27, 1864.
"DEAR SIR,—The Committee appointed by the Selectmen of Dorchester, in accordance with your published suggestions, to obtain in that town contributions for the aid of the loyal sufferers in East Tennessee, feel that in closing their duties they ought to report briefly to yourself.

"They have made personal application to a large number in the town best able to give such charities, many of whom have given with characteristic liberality; and they have caused contributions to be taken up in several of the churches. The amount thus given by the citizens of Dorchester, either through this Committee or otherwise, they find to be about three thousand dollars. And while they would gladly have made this amount larger, they still feel that, if other towns would give in like proportion, an amount will be reached much larger than that originally asked from the State.
"Very respectfully,
"For the Committee,
[Signed] "SAMUEL ATHERTON, *Treas.*"

Brought up $91,123 86		
April 28, Edward Holbrook..	20 00	
" Myrtle Street......	5 00	
" *John W. Peirce, jr., Tremont, Me..	25 00	
" Miss C. R. V.......	2 00	
" Collection in the North Congregational Church and Society at Haverhill, remitted by Mr. Samuel White	162 75	
April 29, Jas. L. Mills & Son.	25 00	
" Mrs. C. R. V.......	2 00	
" Collection in North Congregational Church in Haverhill..............	162 50	
April 30, E. A. H., Roxbury..	15 00	
" Anonymous, in addition to a larger donation........	2 50	
" Collection by the youngest class at M'lle de Bonneville's school for young ladies, 54 Chestnut Street..	25 00	
May 2, A. B..............	4 00	
" Anonymous, a third contribution......	30 00	
" A contribution from		

Carried over......$91,604 61

* The contribution of Master Peirce, a lad of twelve, was remitted in the following letter: —

"S. W. HARBOR, Tremont, Me.,
April 5, 1864.

"DEAR SIR,—Enclosed please find twenty-five dollars, which I have collected for the suffering East Tennesseeans. I had read and heard so much of the sufferings of these loyal people, that I wished very much to do something for them. I said to my mother I will give them my dollar, *all my money.* She said that will do very little good alone, but I might go round and ask my young friends to give for this noble cause. I was pleased to do so, and have collected this sum. I found both old and young ready to give me something; very few refused. In *one* family I got almost five dollars. I know this is a small sum compared with the thousands you are receiving, but if some little boy in each town in this State would go round among his friends, the sums thus collected all put together would make thousands of dollars, and oh! how much suffering would be relieved.
"Respectfully yours,
[Signed] "JNO. W. PEIRCE, Jr."

Brought over....$91,604 61

the citizens of West Amesbury, transmitted by W. J. Boardman, D. M. Tukesbury, and W. F. M. Huntington, Selectmen of Amesbury.... 161 00

May 5,   From the Central Church, Lynn, additional contribution, from P. C. Knapp........... 32 14

"   First Church in Roxbury, Rev. Dr. Putnam, remitted by Mr. S. C. Thwing 933 00

"   North End........ 1 00

"   A Union Boy...... 2 00

"   The proceeds of a little girls' fair in West Cedar St. by Misses Maria Decatur, Grace Kellogg, and Susie Spring.......... 50 65

"   A part of the "Penny Contribution" of the Mather Sabbath School of Jamaica Plain, forwarded by the Superintendent, in accordance with the unanimous wish of the members of the school....... 10 00

"   Anonymous........ 25 00

May 6,   * Lydia S. Gale, a second donation of.............. 100 00

May 7,   Parlor juggling by Ellison & Coolidge........... 2 25

"   * A second contribution of fifty dollars from "A Graft of the Brokers' Board." 50 00

Carried up ...$92,971 65

* The generous donation of Miss Lydia S. Gale was transmitted in the following letter: —

BOSTON, 6th May, 1864.

"SIR, — Being very desirous that the subscription for East Tennessee should amount to one hundred thousand dollars, I again enclose one hundred dollars toward the much wished-for consummation."

Brought up..$92,971 65

May 7,   The North Baptist Society in Dorchester, by the hand of the Pastor, Rev. Mr. Crane.. 15 00

"   Messrs. Nickerson & Co............. 100 00

May 10,   Congregational Ch. and Society of Buckland, forwarded by C. Lord............ 32 10

"   Congregational Society at Acton, Rev. Geo. W. Coleman, Pastor. 7 00

"   Anonymous contribution at St. Paul's Church on Sunday last........ 100 00

"   Balance of a sum contributed by three individuals to defray expenses on a case of caps, vests, &c., prepared by ladies of Beverly, and sent by Miss Hannah C. Adams....... 6 75

"   "Treasurer," — Balance of a fund originally contributed for war purposes. 38 22

"   † Miss Anne Wigglesworth, a second donation of... 100 00

Carried over... $93,370 72

* The contributor who signs himself "A Graft of the Broker's Board," writes:

"I feel that Massachusetts and the whole country are doing too little for those noble and suffering Patriots of East Tennessee. It makes one's blood run cold to hear of what they have to endure. Captain W. W. Dean's published letter is sufficient to urge us on to give more relief. Herewith enclosed is another fifty from "A Graft of the Broker's Board."

† Miss Wigglesworth's second donation was enclosed in the following note: —

"Will Mr. Everett be kind enough to accept the enclosed, that it may lend its little aid in filling the vacuum which exists between the present receipts and the hundred thousand dollars, which we *must* send from Massachusetts.

"I have not waited till this last moment before sending my mite, as my first was sent in February. But I cannot sit still and merely *wish* that our contributions

Brought over.... $93,370 72

May 10, Miss Mary Wigglesworth........... 100 00
May 11, Mr. Emmanuel, an attaché of the Consul-General's office at Constantinople.. 20 00
" Mrs. Albert W. Paine, Bangor, Me....... 10 00
" E. D. Everett...... 20 00
" A lady in Dedham, "her mite,"....... 50 00
" George Eliot Richardson........... 1 00
" Four Cambridge boys 2 00
" A "Boston boy," (one of the first contributors to this fund) third donation..... 10 00
May 12, The earnings of a little boy........... 1 00
" Citizens of Dana, Mass., remitted by N. L. Johnson, chairman of the Selectmen....... 48 65
" Messrs. Faxon, Elms & Co............. 50 00
" Mrs. Peter C. Brooks 200 00
May 13, * J. S. W., one hundred dollars in gold 170 00
" † "Dorchester, 1791," Newton, a second donation of...... 200 00
May 14, Proceeds of an exhibition of tableaux, by four boys; Allen R. Tilden, Vincent Y. Bowditch, J. O.

Carried up.... $94,253 37

should reach the sum of one hundred thousand. I must make my wish — and hope that others will do the same — assume a practical form.
"Very respectfully yours,
"A. WIGGLESWORTH.
"1 Park Street, May 9, 1864."
* J. S. W. writes: — "I enclose you my contribution for the sufferers in East Tennessee. I had hoped, before this, to congratulate you on a completion of the $100,000..... By your letter of yesterday from Dr. Humes, it appears that great destitution still prevails. It is to be hoped that the sum desired from Massachusetts will soon be made up."
† "Dorchester, 1791," writes from Newton as follows:—"The touching evidences we have had of the extreme destitution and suffering of our friends in East Tennessee would seem to demand a division of even the 'crust.'"

9

Brought up..... $94,253 37
S. Huntington and Arthur J. Putnam. 14 30
May 14, Edwin Howland..... 100 00
" Collection taken in the Church of Rev. Samuel Brooks at South Framingham 39 50
" J. Kuhn............ 25 00
" Anonymous 2 00
" B. H.............. 1 00
" M................. 3 00
" A little boy in Woburn............ 1 20
" Henry Lyon, M. D., Charlestown...... 50 00
" † Anonymous, formerly a resident in Knoxville........ 50 00
May 16, Col. Samuel Swett, a second contribution.............. 30 00
" A young lady in Summer Street.... 10 00
" Anonymous......... 10 00
" A lady in Kingston, Mass............. 10 00
" Thos. Wigglesworth, — a second donation of... 100 00
May 17, From a member of the Legislature..... 25 00
" Mrs. A. L. Wales, a second donation of. 50 00
May 18, Amos P. Tapley, Lynn............. 100 00
" Miss Eliza Whitwell, Dorchester......... 100 00
" I. G. R............. 50 00
May 19, What the young Ensign left for the loyal Tennesseeans when he went to serve his country, by H. S. W....,. 5 00
" Isaiah Chase, West Harwich.......... 5 00
May 21, A young lady....... 40 00
" Quincy Sun. School, additional....... 2 00
May 23, Anonymous......... 5 00
" Rev. Alex. Proudfit, Chaplain U. S. A.,

Carried over.... $95,031 37

* The contributor who formerly resided in Knoxville writes: — "Fifty dollars from one who, in days of yore, was a short sojourner about Knoxville, and whose then estimate of East Tennesseans has been borne out and *tested*."

	Brought over....	$95,081 37
	Portsm'th Grove, R. I............	15 00
May 23,	Sam'l Rodman, New Bedford.........	100 00
"	"An Old-Fashioned Man"..........	50 00
May 26,	H. Bromfield Pearson, a second donation.............	50 00
"	Anonymous.......	2 00
"	Proceeds of tableaux by "Ten young ladies of Mr. Shackford's School,"...	25 00
"	The Amesbury Mills Congregational Society.............	37 46
May 28,	George Wilson, New Bedford.........	10 00
"	William Gray, a second donation of...	500 00
"	O. W. Holmes, M.D.	100 00
"	Net proceeds of a musical entertainment at Chickering's Hall, the use of which was given by the Messrs. C.'s gratuitously	1162 00
"	W. H. H. Newman	50 00
"	G. F. H............	5 00
"	Edward Warren, M. D., Newton Lower Falls, (second donation)............	20 00
"	Four school girls at New Bedford.....	7 00
"	Three boys at Walpole, (Arthur Cram, George B. Clark, James B. Lewis,) "the profits of a small store and picking dandelions" in the holidays........	5 00
"	Proceeds of a children's fair, held at the house of William Gray, Esq., by Ellen Gray, Anna Jackson, and Georgiana Eaton..	500 00
May 30,	One day's pay of a Navy Yard employé	3 00
"	Anonymous, Dorchester..........	4 00
"	Congregational Society at Truro, by	
	Carried up.......$97,726 83	

	Brought up	$97,726 83
	the Pastor, Rev. Mr. Noble........	18 00
May 30,	Anonymous, second contribution......	40 00
"	Methodist Society at Malden Centre, by Rev. Mr. Barnes, the Pastor.......	50 50
"	Anonymous gift for East Tennesseans	100 00
May 31,	Addditional from the Methodist Society at Malden Centre, by Rev. Mr. Barnes	20 00
"	Proceeds of a children's fair, held by Georgiana Hayward, Ellen Hayward and Geo. R. R. Rivers. at the house of Dr. Hayward, Temple Place...........	190 00
"	A mite for the poor sufferers in East Tennessee, from a poor female......	5 00
"	Octavius Pickering, a second donation.	30 00
"	"One of the Committee," (a second donation)........	111 00
June 1,	Proceeds of a little child's fair in West Chester Park.....	7 00
"	Mrs. J. Mason Warren..............	100 00
"	Mrs. Charles G. Loring, (a second donation)..........	100 00
June 2,	The proceeds of a gold chain.......	20 00
"	Evelyn, of Norristown, on a visit to Boston..........	5 00
"	Collection at a meeting of the Universalist Society at South Danvers..	33 00
June 2,	Friend X., by the hand of S. E. Sewall, Esq., (a second donation)........	100 00
"	A lady of Roxbury	1 00
"	A member of the State Legislature, who voted against the additional compensation, (a second donation)....	25 00
	Carried over.....$98,682 33	

Brought over,.....$98,682 33

June 2, Hon. S. L. Crocker, Taunton......... 100 00

" Anonymous......... 131 66

" 4, Proceeds of a children's fair at Dr. Talbot's,31 Mount Vernon Street, on Wednesday last..1000 00

" East Tennessee, anonymous 10 00

" Miss Martha B. Waite, remitted by Hon. George B. Upton........... 100 00

" George W. Wales, a second donation.. 100 00

" Mrs. B. C. C. Parker, West Newton 10 00

The following sums remitted by his Honor Jabez C. Knight, Mayor of Providence, R. I., viz :—

June 6, Charles Sherry, Jr., Bristol, R. I...... 100 00

" Ladies' Relief Association, 5th Ward, Providence 100 00

" Joseph A. Barker .. 25 00

" S. G. Mason....... 20 00

" Rev. Dr. Wayland. 25 00

" Charles E. Carpenter.............. 25 00

" Amos D. Smith.... 100 00

" Anonymous........ 10 00

" Several small sums from Olney Arnold, Pawtucket, R. I............. 31 00

" Willy A. Stevens, Cambridgeport, "collected from little playfellows and friends ".... 10 00

June 7, From the Congregational Church and Society in Hollis, N. H...... 56 50

" H. O. H........... 37 98

June 10, Proceeds of a Concert given in the Music Hall on the 4th instant; under the auspices of Mrs. Eastburn... 302 25

" P. B., by the hand of J. J. May....... 10 00

Carried up $100,986 72

Brought up....$100,986 72

June 10, An aged lady who withholds her name, a twenty dollar gold piece.. 39 00

" Proceeds of a collection at the Trinitarian Church at New Bedford, of which Rev. W. Craig is pastor.... 150 00

June 13, Ladies Benevolent Society at North Andover......... 10 00

June 20, Miss Ira E. Loring, a second donation 100 00

" From Misses Mary W.Gannett, Sarah M. Bond, & Grace T. Etheridge, the proceeds of a children's fair 41 25

June 22, Proceeds of an emblematic and dramatic entertainment in Chickering's Hall........ 116 00

June 29, Proceeds of a children's fair, held at the house of John Lowell, Esq., Chestnut Hill, Newton.......... 386 00

July 7, From S. D., by the hand of Rev. Edmund F. Hafter.. 25 00

July 10, W. W. W., Salem.. 8 00

July 13, Small balance of one of the children's fairs 5 00

July 26, First Congregational Church and Society in Yorke, Me. 21 45

Aug. 6, Attleboro' ($128 50) and Wrentham ($41 00) by the hands of Mr. H. Rice 169 50

Aug. 11, Additional from the children's fair, at Dr. Talbot's..... 4 00

Aug. 24, D. B. Check, Danville, Ky......... 5 00

Sept. 17, Capt. S. D. Trenchard, U. S. N...... 20 00

Sept. 21, Miss Jane Bachelor, Northbridge Centre 1 00

Oct. 26, Proceeds of a fair at 109 Pinkney St... 92 16

Total........$102,180 08